A TALE OF
TWO GERMANYS

New Year Celebrations as 1989 turned to 1990 at the Brandenburg Gate — the symbol of German unity at the heart of Berlin. For years inaccessible to ordinary Germans, the gate stood in a closely guarded military area in the East of the city, close to the Berlin Wall. Now the Wall has fallen, the open gate is the symbolic focus of the two Germanys' will to unite again.

A TALE OF
TWO GERMANYS

Text by Martyn Bond
with photographs
by Jons Michael Voss and Volker Döring

atomium books

To all my German friends, in East and West,
who show in their lives that the best of their national
tradition offers hope for the European future.

First published in the United States 1990 by

Atomium Books Inc.
Suite 300
1013 Centre Road
Wilmington, DE 19805.

Layout and cover design: Carl Lauwers
Photo research: Roswitha Gans
Printed in Belgium by Color Print Graphix.

First U.S. Edition
ISBN 1-56182-017-2
EAN 9 781561 820177
2 4 6 8 10 9 7 5 3 1

CONTENTS

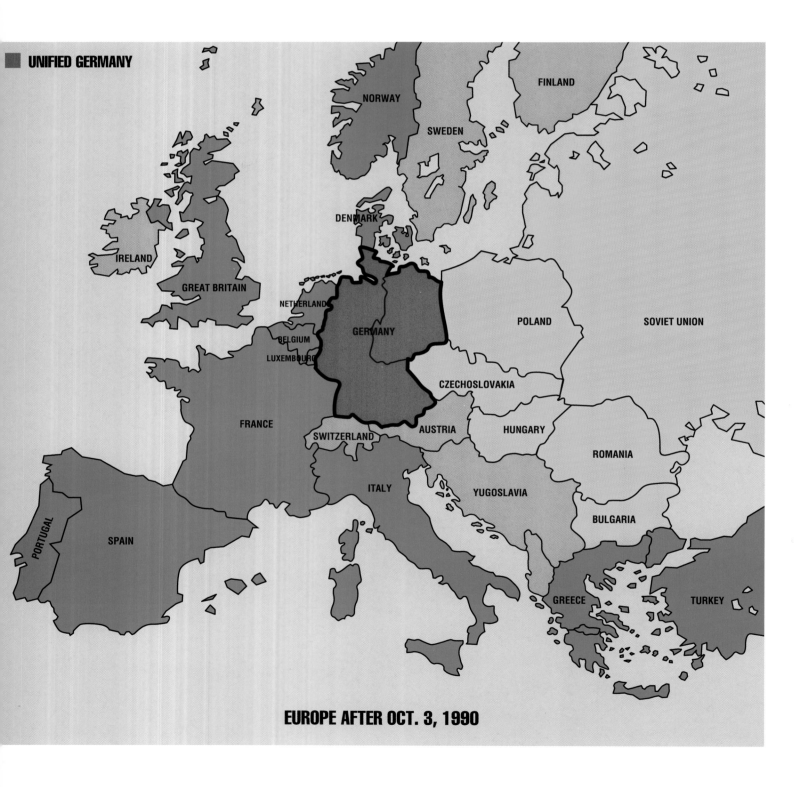

UNIFIED GERMANY

NORWAY

FINLAND

SWEDEN

DENMARK

IRELAND

GREAT BRITAIN

NETHERLANDS

GERMANY

POLAND

SOVIET UNION

BELGIUM

LUXEMBOURG

CZECHOSLOVAKIA

FRANCE

AUSTRIA

HUNGARY

SWITZERLAND

ROMANIA

ITALY

YUGOSLAVIA

PORTUGAL

SPAIN

BULGARIA

GREECE

TURKEY

EUROPE AFTER OCT. 3, 1990

PREFACE

This is a critical moment in history. Revolutionary change is sweeping across the whole of Central and Eastern Europe. Almost every day news breaks of some further reform, a change in law or practice that brings East and West in Europe closer together. A unified Germany is about to appear, the result of a merger of East and West. Given Germany's crucial size, strength, and location, the changes matter there even more than elsewhere.

A Tale of Two Germanys captures this moment with a wealth of photographic detail. A West German photographer toured East Germany, an East German photographer toured West Germany, and with fresh eyes they present their visions of everyday reality.

Their pictures record similarities and contrasts. They show life as it is lived in homes, in schools, in shops, in offices, in factories. The reader can see how much common experience there still is on both sides of the open border, and how much is different. Many of the differences are destined to disappear with the states drawing closer together through monetary union from July 1990 and joint elections the following December. But other differences will remain longer — the contrasts between town and country, between coast and mountain areas, and between the older and the younger generations in East and West. This selection of photographs gives a unique insight into the variety of life in the two Germanys, perhaps at the last moment when many of these distinctions can still be recorded.

As the pace of change accelerates we should not be led astray into judging the direction or importance of change solely by news reports of contemporary events. We all stand on the shoulders of generations who have gone before us. Contemporary Germans, like any other people, are intimately linked to their long and troubled history. What happens today depends on yesterday's events; we cannot understand the present without an awareness of the past. In the case of Germany, understanding that often painful past is of crucial importance not only to Germans themselves but to everyone in the West and the East, from the United States to the Soviet Union, for we will all be affected by future developments in a united Germany.

Thus along with the photographs this book presents a historical review of Germany from its origins up to the postwar development of the two German states, and a contemporary analysis of the events that led to the peaceful revolution in East Germany. The combination of photographs, text, and maps enables the reader to make sense of what is happening now, and to appreciate the changing pattern of daily life as the tale of two Germanys unfolds.

On the map of Europe, the crucial size, strength, and location of unified Germany become apparent.

9

ROME'S EUROPEAN EMPIRE

- ROMAN EMPIRE
- ROMAN INFLUENCE

MARE GERMANICUM

MARE SUEBICUM

BRITANNIA

GERMANIA

BELGICA

GALLIA

DACIA

ILLYRICUM

HISPANIA

ITALIA

MACEDONIA

The Roman Empire at its greatest extent. The German heartlands, east of the Rhine and north of the Danube, remained forever beyond Rome's grasp.

Hermann the Cherusker as he ambushed the Roman legions two thousand years ago and his colossal 19th century monument which towers over the trees near Detmold in the Teutoburg Forest as a symbol of Germany's triumph over Rome.

GERMANY BEFORE THE PEACEFUL REVOLUTION

No country and no people can entirely repudiate their past. Good and bad, light and dark episodes color and disfigure German history. Some are remembered with pride, others suppressed, forgotten. Germanic identity first distinguished itself from other peoples two thousand years ago.

GERMANS AND ROMANS

In his political testament in 14 AD the Emperor Augustus warned his successor never to try to extend the Roman Empire east of the Rhine or north of the Danube into the lands of the Germanic tribes. In earlier years Augustus had sent an army eastward across the Rhine to subdue the barbarian tribes. Hermann, chieftain of the Cherusker, ambushed the Roman general Quintilius Varus and massacred Augustus' three proud legions in the depths of the Teutoburg Forest. That slaughter, at the height of the Roman Empire's power, established the limit of expanding Roman civilization in the Germanic heartlands of Europe.

The Teutoburg Forest lies to the south of what are now the thriving cities of Bielefeld and Detmold, barely 80 miles as the crow flies from the border between what is — or was — East and West Germany. Until the revolution of 1989, that was the Iron Curtain between the democratic West and Communist Eastern Europe, the line where the armies of the invading allies of World War II met over the corpse of Hitler's devastated Germany in 1945.

This land has been Europe's killing fields for centuries. Hermann's massacre of Varus' legions in 9 AD was only a beginning. Four hundred years later Germanic tribes poured across the Rhine, shattering the defenses of an enfeebled Roman Empire and moving on to sack Rome itself. The worship of the gods of the northern forest — Thor, Odin, Freya — overlaid the worship of Roman deities such as Jupiter, Mars, Venus, and Mithras, and came into increasing conflict with the spreading acceptance of Christianity in the decaying empire.

In the centuries that followed, the lands we now know as Germany were the crucible from which came migrating tribes, pressed onward by others from further east, each seeking more space, more fertile lands, until they reached the western edge of Europe at the Atlantic. Angles, Saxons, Jutes, Goths, Visigoths, Alemanni, Franks — often pressed by Slavic tribes close behind them — overran the Celts, romanized Britons, and Gauls, only to intermingle after conquest to create the racial mix, the gene bank of Europe, that makes a mockery of eugenic theories of racial purity in this part of the world.

What eventually flowed back in the opposite direction was the new faith of the conquered. Through the efforts of Christian missionaries — St. Boniface from Britain is the prime example — the pagan tribes were slowly converted, not only in the new lands they had conquered but in their Germanic heartlands as well. Boniface was so successful as a missionary that he earned the title of "Apostle of Germany," but he was martyred for his pains by pagans in Friesland in 754. Often the worship of the old gods lingered on beside the new religion, but slowly faith in a god of mercy rather than gods of vengeance spread through the ambivalent borderlands between the now dismembered Roman Empire in the west and the Slavic kingdoms in the east of Europe.

Modern Germans neither deny nor forget their roots. When Bismarck unified Germany "through

Charlemagne, emperor of the Franks, with the heraldic symbols of Germany (the black eagle) and France (the fleur de lys). Charlemagne's treasure in the cathedral at Aachen bears witness to the extent of his power, which stretched over most of Western Europe some twelve hundred years ago.

blood and iron" in 1870, public subscription completed a two-hundred-foot-high monument to Hermann the Cherusker at the spot in the Teutoburg Forest where he had stopped the march of Rome. Today it is a popular site for outings — a family picnic, a walk in the woods — for scores of thousands of Germans each year. And a chance, conscious or unconscious, for them to be in touch with their roots. History and culture do not die.

CHARLEMAGNE'S LEGACY

Aachen, now the westernmost city in West Germany, is where Charlemagne established his capital. Close to the linguistic border where French, German, and Dutch speakers still live in uneasy harmony, the French call it Aix-la-Chapelle. There Charlemagne's treasure is on display in the cathedral. The architecture is impressive, closely related to the style of Ravenna and Constantinople; and both the treasure and building are richly ornamented with brilliant mosaics, jewels, and imperial gold.

On Christmas Day 800 Charlemagne was crowned emperor of the Franks. The land he ruled came to be known as the Holy Roman Empire, and stretched from the North Sea to the Alps, from the Pyrenees to beyond the Elbe. The title implies a union of Roman tradition, Christian piety, and Germanic temporal power. It needed a man of Charlemagne's energy, vision, courage, and respect

for religion to hold together such a disparate collection of subject peoples, united only in obedience to the emperor and the church.

On his death in 814 the empire was divided between his three sons. The land of the western Franks subsequently became France. The land of the eastern Franks, east of the Rhine, became roughly what was later Germany, though its advancing border with Slavic people further east was in dispute for five hundred years. In between the two lay Lothringen, which retained the capital at Aachen; this elongated north-south territory, which later became the Kingdom of Burgundy, covered roughly what are now the Benelux countries (Netherlands, Belgium, and Luxembourg) and included the provinces of Alsace and Lorraine, and territory further south as far as Switzerland.

Inevitably the sons ruling the eastern and western Franks quarreled with their brother in Lothringen and each attempted to annex his lands to theirs. As so often in politics, envy, cruelty, and greed marked their competition. And their legacy to future generations was a spirit of undying hostility. Both sides subsequently were quite content to overrun what later became the Netherlands, Belgium, and Luxembourg when the opportunity presented itself. In more recent times Alsace and Lorraine have changed hands in war more often than their inhabitants care to remember: in 1870 they fell to Germany; in 1918 they were restored to France; in 1939 they were reconquered by Germany; and in 1945 they were again restored to France.

Thus Lothringen became the western borderlands of the Germans and the eastern borderlands of France. Local dialects remain mostly Germanic, but history has moved the frontiers to and fro. The agricultural resources, the crucial coal and iron deposits, and the strategic situation, offering control of the Rhine and Scheldt rivers, made these borderlands the coveted object of Franco-German enmity.

RELIGION AND POLITICS

German people are more deeply divided by religion than by politics. The division between Catholic and Protestant has been more lasting than any border and it marks ways of thought and behavior that lie deeper than allegiance to any political party or leader.

When Martin Luther, a devout Catholic monk, challenged the religious authorities by nailing his ninety-five theses to the church door in Wittenberg in 1517, he was demanding reform, not revolution. Greater access to humanist education for the growing middle classes in the many small towns had made criticism of a lax and often venal clergy inevitable. The sale of indulgences — a tangible donation of cash in exchange for the intangible remission of penance in Purgatory — was the spark that lit the fire: it looked like a tax on German peasants to finance luxury in Rome.

Where Luther had essentially sought theological reform, the movement that sprang from his teaching demanded social revolution. The Peasants' War that followed brought butchery on a scale not seen for centuries between defenders of the social order and their challengers. The result was an uneasy patchwork of Catholic and Protestant states, each petty prince deciding the religion of his subjects. Within the Holy Roman Empire in Ger-

Martin Luther's challenge to the Church of Rome had consequences far beyond anyone's expectations. From a theological debate it spread to an attack on the established order, a peasants' revolt, and thirty years of religious warfare. The resulting divisions between Catholic and Protestant can still be traced in present-day Germany.

man lands there was guarded tolerance among the princes but intolerance and uniformity of faith inside each little state.

It was a recipe for disaster. Internal rivalries invited intervention from the more homogeneous states surrounding Germany, which itself remained politically divided and weak. The struggle for the souls of the Germans and the territory of German

The Peasants' War, between defenders of the social order and those seeking a social revolution after the Reformation, brought butchery on a scale not seen for centuries.

The sacking of Magdeburg was among the worst excesses of the Thirty Years' War, which set back Germany's development for more than a hundred years.

princes — the Counter-Reformation mounted by the Catholic Church to recoup the losses it suffered through the Reformation — led to bloodshed far more extensive and long-lasting than the Peasants' War. The Thirty Years War from 1618 devastated the country: a third of the population died either in the fighting or from the starvation and disease that followed the breakdown of civil society. When Magdeburg was sacked, nine out of ten of the inhabitants were either killed or driven out to wander the inhospitable countryside. Mercenary armies of mixed nationality, sometimes of one faith, sometimes another, campaigned across Germany, living off the land. Eyewitness accounts record that those who were nominally friends and allies were as evil as the enemy.

The Peace of Westphalia in 1648 imposed an exhausted equilibrium between Catholics and Protestants, but it took close to two hundred years for the country to recover. While the unified nation-states of Britain, the Netherlands, France, Spain, and Portugal expanded overseas and generated wealth through trade, enfeebled Germany had no sense of nationhood, merely local loyalty to a duke, a count, perhaps a city. The Germans' human and financial resources were inadequate for them to engage actively in foreign trade, and internal barriers frustrated manufacture and trade between them. Germany ceased to exist as a cultural concept. The courts of the princes aped foreign manners, dress, and language. It was said in the 18th century of Frederick the Great of Prussia, one of the admirers of the intellectual Enlightenment, that he spoke French to his mistresses, English to his dogs, and German to his servants. Culturally, Germans had become a subject people.

MAKING AND UNMAKING OLD GERMANY

At the end of the 18th century the French Revolution burst on old Germany like a bombshell. Liberty, fraternity, and equality, the ideals of the revolution, were not principles shared by the rulers of the loose collection of one thousand and seven hundred independent states that made up the Holy Roman Empire of German lands. They turned on revolutionary France, which had dared to execute its king, and marched to restore what they deemed legitimate rule. They thought it would be an easy enterprise, their traditional army commanded by aristocrats against a hastily formed and ill-trained assortment from the French peasantry and townfolk. The poet Goethe was with the invading army as it crossed the Rhine and marched into northern France. He watched its ignominious defeat at Valmy in 1793 at the hands of Frenchmen motivated by a patriotism unknown to the German and mercenary troops with their plethora of lesser local loyalties. Goethe wrote that the French cannonade at Valmy would echo down the centuries; here was a different kind of warfare. France was a nation in arms.

Napoleon assumed the inheritance of the revolution and channeled this patriotism into an aggressive expansion of French power. He swept away the Holy Roman Empire, which, as one critic aptly observed, was no longer holy, nor Roman, nor an empire. He annexed to France all the territory west of the Rhine, even extending the French adminis-

trative structure of *départements* along the coast of northern Germany as far as Hamburg. He reshuffled boundaries like a pack of cards, installing one of his brothers as king of the Confederation of the Rhine, a temporary amalgamation of petty German states between that river and the Elbe. Napoleon's radical administrative and social re-

Frederick the Great, architect of Prussian territorial expansion in the 18th century. He made a powerful military machine of his backward, rural kingdom, but not even Prussia could withstand the popular nationalism of revolutionary France. In the Battle of Valmy in 1792, the French defeated a coalition of German states trying to restore the monarchy. The way was open for Napoleon to dominate the continent for the next twenty years.

After Napoleon's defeat, the Great Powers — Russia, Prussia, England and Austria — and smaller German states gathered at the Congress of Vienna to redraw the map of Europe.

The Confederation of the Rhine, Napoleon's amalgamation of petty German states, stretched from the Rhine to the Elbe.

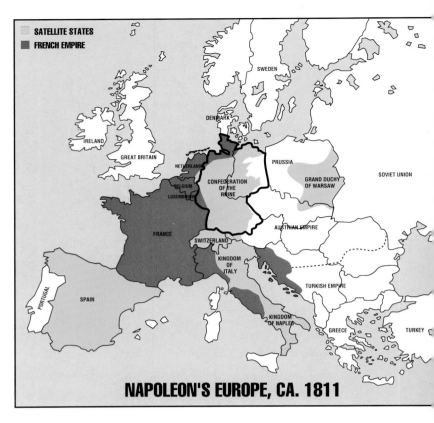

NAPOLEON'S EUROPE, CA. 1811

SATELLITE STATES
FRENCH EMPIRE

forms, often welcomed by progressives, were efficient at raising taxes and troops for his armies. But at his peril he ignored the fact that Germans, like the French before them, were awakening to the idea of nationhood and sensing the patriotism that accompanied it.

In 1812 Napoleon overextended himself militarily and had to beat a costly retreat from Moscow in the face of a bitter winter and a vengeful Russian army. His former German allies rose against him, fired by a new enthusiasm for things Germanic, from history and folksong to architecture and language. In 1813 Napoleon was resoundingly defeated at Leipzig in the Battle of the Nations — a significant name — and sued for peace. He broke the terms of the peace two years later when he escaped from exile and rallied his troops to fight, but he lost yet again, this time to a combined British and Prussian force at Waterloo. It was, as the victorious Duke of Wellington said, "the nearest run thing you ever saw." But essentially the die had been cast two years before at Leipzig. Germany was at last on the move, both as an idea and as a powerful force in European affairs, and Napoleon was the first to feel the effects.

The ministers who gathered at the Congress of Vienna to settle the shape of Europe after the Napoleonic wars were in agreement about one thing: the danger of subversive republican ideas allied to powerful emotions of national identity. They had

seen the destruction wreaked by revolutionary France; the last thing they wanted was a German version of the same phenomenon. Napoleon had swept away the Holy Roman Empire; in its place the Congress of Vienna created the German Confederation. It was a loose association of sovereign states of very different sizes, a far cry from the unitary national state German radicals were agitating for. Under the reactionary leadership of Prussia and Austria, the confederation suppressed all aspirations for unity. Rigid censorship and close control of the universities stifled efforts to secure social and political freedoms. This ensured that conservative forces associated with the name of Metternich, the chief Austrian minister, guided the political destiny of German lands — until the pent-up forces of revolution broke out explosively in 1848.

1848: PROMISE BETRAYED

The dominant political forces in Germany in the 19th century were undoubtedly conservative, often reactionary. But economic developments were shaping practical changes that worked against these politically reactionary tendencies. In 1834 a German customs union was established, creating a unitary inland market. In 1835 the first German railway line was opened. Industries spread fast and a growing class of factory workers swelled the population of the larger towns. In 1844 starving

Silesian weavers went on strike. They were ruthlessly suppressed by Prussian troops, but the industrial working class had begun to organize.

The revolution of 1848, however, was as much a revolt by the middle classes against politically reactionary princes as an uprising of the working class against an exploitative industrial system. Although the Communist Manifesto of Karl Marx and Friedrich Engels dates from this year of revolutions, the Communists' role in the uprisings was marginal. Revolution spread from Paris in February to the German states the following month. The middle classes rose to claim a share in government and the frightened princes conceded written constitutions where previously they had ruled with arbitrary authority.

A National Assembly met in Frankfurt to draft a constitution for all Germany. It was dominated by Liberal (centrist) parliamentarians who aimed not for universal suffrage but only a limited vote. They feared anarchy from the democratic left more than the re-establishment of the old governing powers. When Austrian interests tried to insist on a "greater Germany," including many non-German-speaking nations of its empire, a majority in the assembly supported a "smaller Germany" that excluded Austria completely. They offered the crown of their newly created country to the king of Prussia, Frederick William IV. He scathingly refused it, saying he would not owe his crown to an illegitimate assembly sprung from a revolution.

Popular uprisings in May 1849 in Baden,

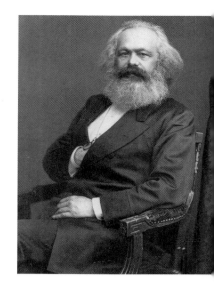

Karl Marx, German journalist and political thinker, whose collaboration with Friedrich Engels produced the Communist Manifesto in 1846. His main work, Das Kapital, *appeared in 1867, and he died in 1883.*

Saxony, and the Rhineland then gave the reactionaries their opportunity. The princes put down the uprisings with exemplary brutality. The assembly was dissolved at the point of the bayonet. The constitutions of individual states were revised to put the clock back. Attempts to set Germany along a path to unity through parliamentary democracy had failed. The alternative was unity realized by force of arms. This Bismarck achieved brilliantly, but at immense human cost "through blood and iron," in the decade from 1862 to 1871.

Otto von Bismarck, credited with forging German unity "through blood and iron," governed Prussia from 1860 until his dismissal by the new Emperor, Wilhelm II, in 1890.

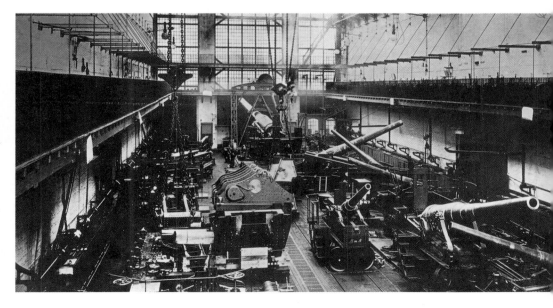

BISMARCK AND THE GERMAN REICH

Otto von Bismarck became prime minister of Prussia in 1862. The Prussia he governed stretched across northern Germany from the Rhineland in the west to the town of Königsberg on the Baltic in the east, now the Soviet city of Kaliningrad. The Rhineland gave Prussia industrial power through the coal and iron of the Ruhr; the eastern provinces supplied an agricultural surplus. Prussia's size gave it an army that was the envy and the dread of its less extensive neighbors. Bismarck governed this industrious and well-organized state without the annual parliamentary approval of the budget that the constitution required, but he had the confidence of the king, and foreign policy successes gave him a popularity with the people that he was denied in the parliament.

In 1864 Prussia, in alliance with Austria, defeated Denmark and seized the duchies of Schleswig and Holstein (now the northernmost region of West Germany). For two years the victors administered the provinces jointly, then Bismarck attacked and defeated Austria. This enabled him to annex Schleswig-Holstein to Prussia and to eliminate Austrian influence in the struggle for authority over the lesser German states. He then gathered together the states north of the river Main and established the North German Federation, in which Prussia was the dominant power.

His next act of aggression was against France, in a war he engineered over a diplomatic incident concerning the succession to the Spanish throne. At Sedan, German troops routed the French army and captured the French emperor, a nephew of Napoleon I. Bismarck's troops entered Paris and as a crowning insult to the defeated French, he proclaimed King Wilhelm I of Prussia to be German emperor in a ceremony at Versailles in the famous Hall of Mirrors in January 1871.

Bismarck had united the "smaller Germany" without Austria. Territorially this was the Germany the National Assembly had dreamed of in 1848, but he had united it by force of arms and economic domination, not by popular consent. Prussia dominated the empire. Despite universal suffrage and the appearance of formal democracy in the Imperial Assembly, the real decisions were made in the Federal Council by the representatives of the ruling princes of the member states. Bismarck as

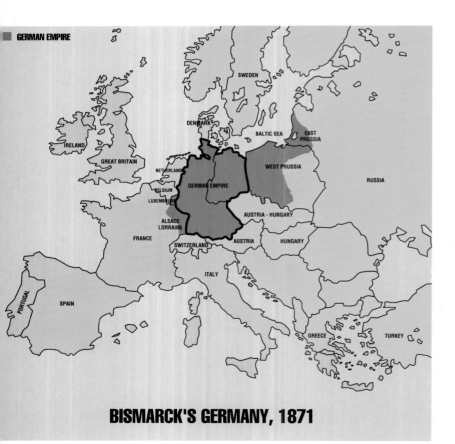

BISMARCK'S GERMANY, 1871

Proclamation of King Wilhelm I of Prussia as German Emperor in the Hall of Mirrors in Versailles in January 1871. Bismarck stands center-stage in white.

Guided by Bismarck, the German Empire dominated the map of north-central Europe, and Germany at last became a nation-state, respected and feared by its neighbors.

chancellor was responsible not to the assembly but to the emperor.

Bismarck governed the German Empire until 1890, vainly trying to head off the growing working class's demands for social justice and the Catholic Church's demands for religious and educational freedom. Despite progressive social security and health laws, the workers were alienated by legislation banning their political organization, the Social Democratic Party. The Catholic Church was alienated by being given the appearance of power without the substance, especially in education.

Bismarck's creation of a "benevolent dictatorship" had all the trappings of success: Germany was a nation-state at last, respected and feared by its neighbors. But its strength rested on insecure supports. The system of government was tolerable only while it was successful; too few citizens had any real stake in it, economically or politically, for it to survive the storms that were soon to overtake it.

FROM POWER TO IMPOTENCE, FROM EMPIRE TO DEFEAT

Within less than two years of succeeding his father, Emperor Wilhelm II, eager to assert his authority, "dropped the pilot" in 1890, as a famous cartoon in *Punch* described it. Without Bismarck's foresight the young and vacillating emperor was no match for the short-term vested interests of those who benefited from the industrial, agricultural, and military might of Germany. From 1890 to 1914 Germany's economic strength, population growth, technological advance, and expansion of trade were exceptional. But the land-owning *Junkers* (Prussian aristocrats) and industrialists wanted ever larger profits and markets. To German opinion it seemed that the older European powers were blocking the way, monopolizing colonies, denying Germany its place in the sun. The Germans felt blocked by the multinational Austro-Hungarian Empire in the south, France and Britain in the west, and Russia in the east. The officer class was impatient. Europe drifted to war in 1914, and Germany thought it would gain from the conflict.

It is a tribute to Germany's strength and energy at the time of World War I that its armies came

Poison gas and machine guns slaughtered the flower of a generation in World War I, 1914-1918. The western front stretched from the North Sea to neutral Switzerland, but the carnage was worst in the trenches in Flanders and northern France. US involvement in 1917 turned the tide against Germany, which forfeited US sympathy when a U-Boat torpedoed the liner Lusitania with the loss of hundreds of lives on a voyage from New York to Liverpool in 1915.

close to crushing the combined might of Russia, France, and Britain on two separate fronts. Unwisely, the German High Command provoked the United States to enter the war in April 1917, just as the Russian armies were collapsing. The tide of war changed on the western front. That year a far-sighted majority in the Reichstag voted for a negotiated peace without annexation, but the members of the High Command ignored the democratic vote. In March 1918 they imposed the Treaty of Brest-Litovsk on the new Soviet government, annexing a

The harsh terms of the peace treaty following World War I contributed to hyperinflation in Germany. Prices were astronomic, bank notes were valued by weight, and even used by children as toy building bricks. Poverty bred despair and political extremism.

swathe of Eastern Europe with fifty-five million inhabitants from Finland to the Ukraine. It was an expression of a will to dominate all of Eastern Europe, a will expressed even more forcibly by the Nazis a generation later.

In the west, U.S. involvement ensured an Allied victory. The German High Command retreated, then demanded that the politicians it had

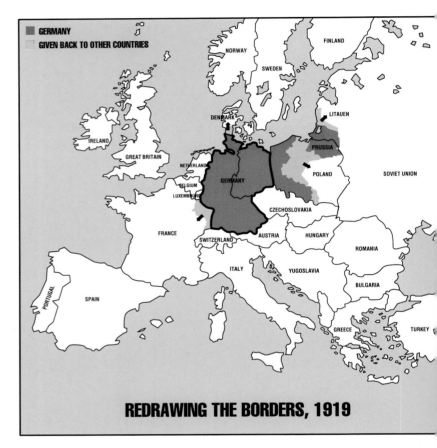

REDRAWING THE BORDERS, 1919

previously ignored should sue for peace, neatly absolving the military of guilt in Germany's defeat. The emperor abdicated and went into exile in the Netherlands. Germany became a republic. But the terms of the Treaty of Versailles dictated by the Allies, in particular the vengeful French leader, Clemenceau, ensured that the new political leadership in Germany would be unpopular. The National Assembly that met in Weimar faced the loss of Alsace-Lorraine to France, the port of Schleswig to Denmark, and Silesia and part of the Baltic coast to Poland. On top of that Germany had to pay huge sums in reparation for war damage, and suffered military occupation of the Rhineland. The democratic parties in the new Weimar Republic had a popular majority in the assembly, but extreme nationalist opinion on the right and extreme socialist opinion on the left harried the democrats in their efforts to restore Germany to the family of nations. Political assassination and terror became widespread. The army remained disaffected, feeling stabbed in the back by politicians who had agreed to what many saw as dishonorably severe peace terms.

Against this background, made worse by the Great Crash of 1929, political and military intrigues paved the way for the takeover by the National Socialists — the Nazis — in 1933. "The best lack all conviction, while the worst are full of passionate intensity," the Irish poet William Butler Yeats had written a few years after World War I. It could serve as an epitaph for Weimar Germany.

BARBARISM AND TECHNOLOGY: NAZI GERMANY

In formal terms, World War II started in September 1939 when Germany invaded Poland, bringing France and Britain into conflict with the aggressor because of their mutual defense pact with Hitler's victim. But in another sense it began as soon as Adolf Hitler came to power, for what the Nazi movement stood for was the antithesis of what the bourgeois democracies represented. Confrontation was inevitable.

Hitler soon rid himself of the few conservative allies who had helped him into power. He intimidated the Reichstag to the point where it approved an act giving him exceptional powers, then banned all parties except his. He eliminated political opponents from the civil service, the teaching profession, and the press. He brought the Protestant churches into line by encouraging a German Christian movement that was politically obedient to his will. He smashed the trade unions ruthlessly and abolished many civic rights. Thousands of his opponents disappeared, some in street violence, some into concentration camps.

Step by step the regime put its anti-Semitic policy into practice. Jews were harassed, their businesses boycotted, synagogues burned; they were banned from the professions, forbidden to teach. Finally they were herded into camps and systematically murdered. More than six million Jews from Germany and from the lands the Nazis conquered died before the end of the war. Other victims included political opponents of the Nazis, especially Communists and Social Democrats, as well as racial and social minorities such as Gypsies, homosexuals, and the mentally handicapped.

After World War I, the Treaty of Versailles broke up the German Empire, severely cutting back its borders and in the process ensuring the unpopularity of the Weimar government.

Faced with the extremes of Communism on the Left and the Nazis on the Right, the impoverished electorate voted increasingly for Hitler's National Socialists. He was supported by several industrialists and later endorsed by the army.

Loyalty to the Nazis had its counterpart in hostility toward an enemy: Jews were seen as the "enemy within." A boycott of Jewish businesses led to better business for German shops. When vast crowds in Vienna welcomed Hitler's takeover of Austria in 1938, he declared his "civilizing mission" in Slav lands. After two years of a cynical "nonaggression pact" with Stalin, he launched the German army against the Soviet Union in 1941.

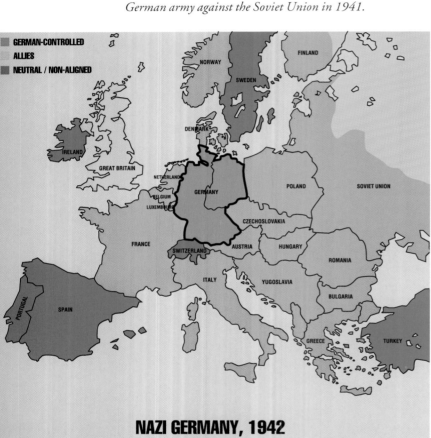

GERMAN-CONTROLLED
ALLIES
NEUTRAL / NON-ALIGNED

NAZI GERMANY, 1942

At the height of Nazi Germany's power in 1942, the territory it controlled extended from Norway as far south as Greece, and from France to the gates of Moscow.

The world saw the assembled might of the SS at the Nuremberg Rallies, but not the huddled masses in the concentration camps whose names are a litany of accusation against the Nazi regime: Buchenwald, Dachau, Auschwitz, Treblinka . . .

Most Germans accepted developments under Hitler without objecting or resisting. Democracy and the idea of a country ruled by law in the interests of all its members had not taken root in the short, turbulent years of the Weimar Republic. The loss of rights seemed to be compensated by an improvement in the material standard of living. Unemployment was virtually eliminated. And, as under Bismarck, a series of foreign policy successes strengthened the regime's popularity. In 1935 the Saar region was restored to Germany, in 1938 Austria was merged with Germany, and in the same year the Sudetenland was taken from Czechoslovakia. Popular enthusiasm for the Nazis was demonstrated at mass rallies and relayed by a sophisticated propaganda machine.

From the start Hitler had plans to conquer all of Europe. He claimed German superiority over all neighboring peoples and in September 1939 he invaded Poland to prove it. Hitler was secure in the knowledge that a secret pact signed with Stalin ensured that the Soviet Union would not come to Poland's assistance. On the contrary, Stalin was free to annex the Baltic states of Lithuania, Latvia, and Estonia and even parts of eastern Poland in exchange for leaving Hitler a free hand in the bulk of Poland. The deal served both their purposes. Each knew he was cynically buying time and gaining territory, but the big showdown had to come. It did in 1941, when Hitler launched a major attack on the Soviet Union and, like Napoleon before him, reached the gates of Moscow.

During the five and a half years of World War II, German armies defeated Poland, Denmark, Norway, the Netherlands, Belgium, France, Yugoslavia, and Greece. In the Soviet Union they rolled the Russians back to Moscow, and in North Africa they threatened Egypt and the Suez Canal. The technological superiority of German arms carried the day until 1942, when the tide turned. German forces were overextended and opposition, especially in the Soviet Union, was more determined than Hitler expected. From 1942 on, the Axis of Germany, Italy, and Japan began to suffer defeats in all theaters of the war. As in World War I, U.S. involvement was decisive. In 1943 the Allies landed in Italy, and the following year in Normandy. Slowly German forces retreated from their posi-

Like Napoleon and the French one hundred and thirty years before them, the Germans failed to conquer Russia. The Soviet army defeated them at Stalingrad in 1943, taking scores of thousands of prisoners. After two more years of bitter fighting, Soviet troops reached Berlin. Hitler committed suicide as they closed in on his command bunker, and the city fell after weeks of street-by-street fighting.

tions in the south and in the west. And in the east their troops were also retreating before the overwhelming numbers of the Soviet Red Army.

In July 1944 disaffected German officers with some civilian support attempted a coup but failed. Hitler ruthlessly pursued any opposition, and a wave of savage repression followed the failure of the Stauffenberg plot. Doggedly, Hitler continued the war despite enormous losses, until the whole of the Reich was occupied by invading armies. While the Red Army was battling for Berlin in April 1945, Hitler committed suicide, leaving orders that the city was to be defended to the last man. Eight days later an unconditional surrender was signed.

The war in Europe cost close to fifty million lives. Germany suffered the worst defeat in its history: most towns lay in ruins, a quarter of all houses were destroyed, the most urgent essentials of life were lacking. Millions of Germans were captives, millions more were homeless, millions were in flight as refugees before the invading armies. The amoral alliance of technology with Nazi claims to dominance had brought Germany to its knees — materially ruined and a moral outcast from the family of nations.

* * *

Before the division of Germany in 1945, the two German states shared this common history. Yet until recently, historical exhibitions in East Germany and West Germany interpreted that history in diametrically opposed ways.

In East Berlin the main display in the Historical Museum showed a resolutely Marxist interpretation of German history, stressing the role of the working class and Communist organizers. Until free elections in 1990, the East German exhibition culminated in a huge tableau portraying the "liberation" of Berlin by the Red Army in 1945. In West Berlin the historical exhibition in the Reichstag concentrates on the brief periods of parliamentary democracy in German political history and emphasizes the role of capital, entrepreneurs, and innovators. It is hard to believe these displays refer to the history of the same Germany, the common ancestor of the two countries. As the two Germanys unite, their reinterpretation of their common and their uncommon histories will be the key to how people of the next generation make use of the added strength that unity gives them.

POSTWAR GERMANY: TWO PHOENIXES FROM THE ASHES

Look for the Germany that collapsed in ruins in 1945 and you will not find it on the map. The victorious Allies redrew the boundaries, abolishing old Prussia and apportioning more than forty thousand square miles — East Prussia, Silesia, part of Pomerania, and Brandenburg — to the Soviet Union and Poland. Even before the 1945 Potsdam Declaration by Stalin, Truman, and Churchill, four million Germans had left these eastern territories, fleeing before the Red Army. More than five million others followed them, expelled after the Potsdam decision. Three million more were expelled from the Sudetenland when it was restored to Czechoslovakia. Germany shrank, its borders moved westward, and refugees flooded into the truncated country.

The colossal burden of more than twelve million refugees, most of whom settled in the British

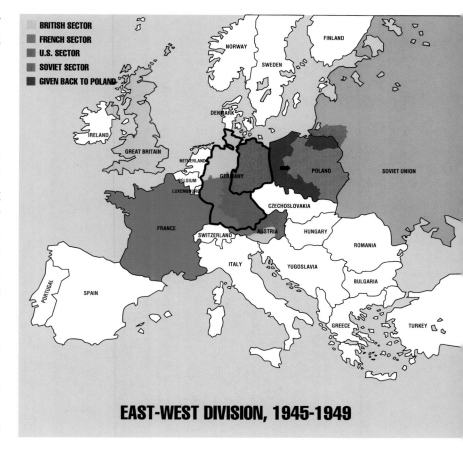

EAST-WEST DIVISION, 1945-1949

Again the victors redrew Germany's boundaries; its borders moved westward, and by the end of 1949, two separate German states had been created.

More than twelve million Germans were refugees in the immediate postwar period. They flooded back into what was left of Germany as its borders were redrawn, ceding large tracts of territory to the Soviet Union, Poland, and Czechoslovakia. In the devastated cities the slow and painful work of reconstruction began.

and U.S. zones of occupation, strained the resources of the shattered German economy. Initially the Allies planned to strip the conquered country of industries, to ensure that Germany would never rebuild the economic power to dominate the con-

The Soviet blockade of Berlin from June 1948 to May 1949 tested the Western Allies' resolve to maintain the freedom of the Western sectors of the city. The Allies' continuous airlift of supplies won the allegiance of the defeated Germans.

tinent again. But the British, French, and American occupying authorities soon reversed this policy in their sectors. James Byrnes, the U.S. secretary of state, wrote at the time: "Germany is part of Eu-

rope and recovery in Europe, particularly in the states adjoining Germany, will be slow indeed if Germany with her great resources of coal and iron is turned into a poorhouse." The British economist John Maynard Keynes had seen the same problem a generation earlier and criticized excessive reparation demands after World War I. He wrote then in his polemical book, *The Economic Consequences of the Peace*: "Round Germany as a central support the rest of the European economic system grouped itself, and on the prosperity and enterprise of Germany the prosperity of the rest of the continent mainly depended."

Realizing this, the Western Allies included their occupation zones in the Marshall Plan, which reinvigorated the war-torn economies of the non-Communist countries of Western Europe with U.S. dollar grants and loans. The Soviet Union refused the offer of Western aid for its occupation zone. Growing rivalry between the Soviet Union, with its Communist system of government in the East, and the Western world, with its democratic system, divided Germany and Berlin, a four-power "island" in the middle of the Soviet occupation zone. When the Soviet Union imposed a road and rail blockade on the western sectors of Berlin in the summer of 1948, the Allies responded with an extensive airlift that lasted almost a year. Food, fuel, clothing, even building materials were flown to the beleaguered city to maintain more than a million civilians and the Allied garrisons. The Soviet Union could not gain the support of the Berliners and it could not starve them into surrender. The battle was on between East and West for the hearts and minds of the Germans, and the battle line of this "cold war" ran through the middle of their country.

By the end of 1949, within months of the lifting of the Berlin blockade, there were two separate states, East and West Germany, each the creation of rival occupying powers. The Federal Republic of Germany, which took Bonn as its capital, was based on Western values of parliamentary democracy, legal security, civil liberties, human rights, private property, and private enterprise. The German Democratic Republic, with its capital in East Berlin, was based on socialist principles. There the Communist Party (with which the numerically stronger Social Democratic Party had been forced to merge in 1946) was the dominant force in society, and the government owned and controlled the essential means of production and distribution.

Two countries so different in fundamental values made uncomfortable neighbors. Their hostility was worsened by the presence of the most heavily armed alliances the world has ever seen — the North Atlantic Treaty Organization (NATO) and the Warsaw Pact — whose heaviest concentrations of arms and men were stationed on German soil.

Individual freedoms in the West acted as a powerful magnet to Germans in the East. From 1952 East Germany began to construct an elaborate barbed-wire fence and lay minefields along the border with the West. This death strip finally extended for nearly a thousand miles, from the Baltic to the Czechoslovakian frontier. As the border between the two Germanys was sealed off, would-be refugees flocked to Berlin to cross the still-open boundary with the Allies' sectors and then fly to freedom. Three and a half million East Germans took this route before it, too, was closed, in August 1961: the Communist authorities, desperate to retain the skilled workers on whom the economy relied, built the Berlin Wall. It became a symbol of the bankruptcy of a system that could not convince its own people to stay in their country.

RECONSTRUCTION

Each of the Germanys has had its successes and failures. Both began from the ashes of defeat and built themselves into the countries we see today, or saw until so recently. Occupation by the Allies was certainly no picnic, but for most Germans it was preferable to occupation by the Red Army, as the flood of refugees moving westward proved at the end of the war. Marshall Plan aid and currency reform in the West were preferable to industrial dismantling in the East. West Germany also had more population, more territory, and richer natural resources than the East, giving it a head start in reconstruction. But the nature of reconstruction was determined by social, economic, and personal factors specific to each of the Germanys.

Each of the two German states was very quickly embedded in the economic and military alliances of East and West. West Germany was a founding

member of the European Community, or Common Market; East Germany was a founding member of Comecon, the Soviet-bloc equivalent. West Germany became the dominant non-nuclear member of NATO; East Germany assumed the

The Berlin Walls, built in 1961, was a visible admission of failure by the East German regime to persuade its people to stay in their own country voluntarily. Even the workers sent to build it were watched and guarded by well armed militiamen to prevent them from fleeing to the West.

same role in the Warsaw Pact. The prospect of the two "halves" of Germany ever growing together again in peace seemed remote. In any case they

Konrad Adenauer, first Chancellor of West Germany from 1949 to 1963, represented continuity with a German tradition that predated the Nazis. He had been mayor of Cologne during the Weimar Republic but the Nazis had removed him from office in 1933. After the war leading Nazis were brought to trial at Nüremberg and sentenced for crimes against humanity.

would be dependent on changing relations between the superpowers.

The first West German chancellor, Konrad Adenauer, understood this well. He saw West Germany as an integral part of the Western alliance. A Rhinelander, a Catholic, and already an old man when he came to power, Adenauer was naturally suspicious of the Prussian, Protestant, and socialist traditions strong in German history. It suited him to establish a "provisional" capital in Bonn, a small, provincial town far removed from the associations

and influences of Berlin. As long as he was at the helm, he considered his main task to be ensuring the acceptance of West Germany in the eyes of the Allies and other Western neighbors, making his German state respectable again in the family of nations. The culmination of his work was the treaty of cooperation between France and Germany signed in 1963, the year of his retirement. The economic success of West Germany under his leadership was such that when he retired at age 87, commentators could speak of his creation, West Germany, as an economic giant even if it was still a political dwarf.

One of Adenauer's achievements was to establish democratic institutions in West Germany that would survive any battering from extremist forces. The threat of political extremism led to the banning of the rightist Socialist Reichs Party in 1952 and of the German Communist Party in 1956. The Christian Democrats under Adenauer developed into a catchall party of the right, which weakened the appeal of extreme-right groups. The Social Democratic Party performed a similar function on the left, after its reformist conference in Godesburg in 1959. Until the arrival of the environmentalist Greens in the 1980s, the liberal Free Democrats were the only viable alternative, with electoral support varying from 5 percent to 10 percent.

In the West, the process of de-Nazification in the immediate postwar period was limited by what was perceived as a need to rebuild the occupied zones into a functioning country. After the trial of major war criminals at Nuremberg, teachers, lawyers, civil servants, and even soldiers associated with the defeated regime were brought back quickly into active professional life through re-education programs. A concern for efficiency overrode concern for ideological purity; West Germany was conceived as a pluralist and tolerant state.

In the East, de-Nazification was a more thoroughgoing process, inspired as much by ideological fervor as by a desire to settle accounts. The avowed goal of the occupying power was not parliamentary democracy but a dictatorship of the proletariat under the leadership of the Communist Party. In the industrial areas in the south of the Soviet zone — Leipzig, Dresden, Bitterfeld, Jena — and in East Berlin the Social Democratic tradi-

President Kennedy confirmed U.S. support for a free West Berlin on an official visit in 1963: "Ich bin ein Berliner."

Massive demonstrations in front of West Berlin's town hall were witness to the warmth of German support for the U.S. presence.

tion was strong, so the Communist Party forced through a merger with the Social Democrats in 1946 in order to harness this support. The resulting Socialist Unity Party (or SED, to use its German abbreviation) has dominated East Germany ever since and is often commonly referred to as the Communist Party. Other parties were not banned, and were even actively supported, as long as they acknowledged the leading role of the SED. Hence small Christian, liberal, national, and farm parties existed in close collaboration with the SED, but they did not campaign against it with truly alternative policies. They were simply fronts, designed to be more acceptable faces of the system turned either outward for international consumption or inward to bring particular sections of domestic opinion into line with Communist policy.

Consequently, until the revolution of 1989, election results in East Germany were a foregone conclusion. In West Germany, on the other hand, a shift of a few percentage points in either direction was and still is enough to change the government from Social Democratic to Christian Democratic. In forming a government there, the additional seats of the Free Democrats have often been crucial to one party or the other.

OPPOSITION

Political opposition has not been restricted to parliamentary opposition. In both countries,

though under very different conditions, groups unable to express their points of view within national or local parliamentary structures have resorted to alternative means of protest.

When the two major parties in West Germany joined together in government as the "Grand Coalition" from 1966 to 1969, extraparliamentary opposition centered on the student movement. Initially demanding reforms in schools and universities, the movement soon widened its concerns to foreign affairs, particularly the U.S. policy in Vietnam and West German relations with reactionary regimes in the Third World. In 1968, street demonstrations were violently dispersed by the police and a student leader was killed. The Bundestag, the parliament in Bonn, put emergency powers into effect, triggering massive protests across the country against excessive government power and the conservative social structure of West Germany and its institutions.

The mass demonstrations died away as educational changes and progressive social legislation were introduced. But for a hard core of people opposed to the government and its institutions, the problems raised by the extraparliamentary opposition were not to be solved by simply amending laws. Terrorism was the answer of these extremists to what they saw as repressive and reactionary state control. West Germany was confronted with this challenge through the 1970s and 1980s. Terrorist attacks reached a peak in 1977 with the murders of the federal prosecutor, a leading banker, and the president of the Employers' Federation, and the hijacking of a plane belonging to the national airline, Lufthansa. The East German secret police played a supporting role, giving safe haven, money, and even training to terrorists. But tough security action in the West, at the outer limit of what many could accept in a democratic society, stemmed the tide of terrorism, even though the price was alienation of some of the younger generation from the democratic process. While the problem of terrorism did not go away, it was reduced to proportions that did not destabilize the country.

In East Germany the Communist Party permeated the state. Control of political power by what was ostensibly the workers' party was the reason for the government's existence. Open political protest inevitably challenged the very raison d'être of the state. By definition the people could not have interests different from those of the party that governed in their name. So in June 1953, party and state were shaken to their foundations when building workers in East Berlin went on strike to protest an enforced increase in their prescribed work load. The spontaneous strike spread quickly across the city; columns of workers marched to the Brandenburg Gate. Workers in other cities struck and took to the streets. The movement gathered pace over five hectic days. As it got out of hand, the German Communist authorities appealed to the

The rising in East Berlin in June 1953 was put down by Soviet tanks, exposing the weakness of the regime's popular support. In West Germany radical groups degenerated into terrorism and found some sympathy among intellectuals, but no widespread support in the population.

Soviet occupying forces, who brutally suppressed the rebellion with tanks.

The rising exposed the weakness of East Germany's foundations. The government and party were meant to be the expression of the workers' will; now they were shown to be merely the cloak of the occupying army, an unpopular regime maintained by force. The lesson was not lost on the Communist Party, which strengthened internal security. Nor was it lost on the people, who learned they had to deal not only with their German government but, behind it, the interests of the Soviet Union. It was a lesson repeated in Hungary in 1956 and in Czechoslovakia in 1968. Not until the very end of the 1980s was the situation to change.

ENVIRONMENTAL PROBLEMS

Environmental protest was common to both Germanys, though articulated in quite different ways. In the West, large and often violent demonstrations against the building of nuclear power stations, highways, or airport runways brought police and demonstrators into open conflict. Concern for the effects of acid rain and polluted rivers mobilized thousands of citizens. "Green" opinion found expression not only in demonstrations but in the parliamentary process, with successes for Greens in local government elections in the late 1970s and in the Bundestag in the 1980s. But in East Germany, protest by small groups concerned about appalling abuses of the environment by industry was nipped in the bud by the Stasi, the secret police, for whom any criticism of conditions in East Germany was an attack on the socialist system.

Protesters in East Germany found the opportunity to express their opinions only within the framework of the church, as all other avenues were directly controlled by the government and the Communist Party, which ran the government with a monopoly on political power. Protest centered on the degraded environment, the militarization of schooling, the refusal of the government to make adequate provision for conscientious objectors, the growing threat of nuclear escalation, the illiberal cultural policy, and above all people's inability to travel outside East Germany, especially to the West.

Those who protested took major personal risks. The Stasi exercised far-reaching control of society on behalf of the Communist Party. It is estimated that between eighty-five thousand and one hundred and twenty thousand full-time members of the secret police "ran" a further one million part-time informers in a population of only sixteen million. When Stasi records were opened in 1990, files on more than four million citizens were discovered. Against this almost impenetrable information network, small, isolated groups of protesters could make no headway without the support of the churches.

THE ROLE OF THE CHURCHES

The underlying religious divisions in Germany reflect the division of the country at the time of the Reformation and the Counter-Reformation. That left essentially a Protestant North and East, and a Catholic South and West. But waves of refugees and the movement of population from rural areas into the cities blurred this simple picture. Now both groups are found throughout the land, though majorities in different areas still reflect the old divisions.

Hence, in West Germany Protestants and Catholics are approximately equal in number, with Catholics more numerous in the south (Bavaria) and in the Rhineland. The churches there, like so many other social institutions, had to be rebuilt after 1945, not only materially but also spiritually. With a few notable exceptions they had gone along with the Nazi regime and in some cases even supported it with enthusiasm. In the postwar reconstruction, however, the churches in the West offered an alternative and ostensibly apolitical structure that fit into the Allies' conception of a pluralist society. Like free trade unions and employers' organizations, like a variety of press and media institutions, the churches could articulate some of the varied attitudes that make up society. So vital were they considered that a "church tax" was levied on all employed people and divided among the main faiths in accordance with the wishes of the taxpayers, who could opt for one or the other. As a result the West German churches became not only wealthy but pillars of the rebuilt social order.

In East Germany, the Lutheran Church boasts approximately four million adherents, more than four times the membership of the Roman Catholic Church. For thirty years after the founding of East Germany, the two church communities fought a losing battle against the atheistic Communist state. The battleground was the field of education. Despite dramatic gestures, such as that of a pastor who burned himself to death in 1976 to protest indoctrination of East German youth, the state conceded nothing to the church. The East German youth initiation ceremonies (*Jugendweihe*) were reminiscent of Hitler youth ceremonies, designed to foster loyalty to a state founded on materialist, not spiritual, principles. The church was totally excluded from them; indeed, they formed the state's response, and alternative, to the tradition of Christian Confirmation. The churches found themselves becoming antagonistic and impotent, relegated to a shrinking pastoral role, without any influence on the conduct of public affairs.

The Lutheran Church, after much internal discussion, declared in 1978 that it would no longer be a church *against* the socialist state or even outside it, but would seek a role *inside* socialism. In an understanding with the Communist Party, the church undertook the care of those marginalized by society. This was supposed to mean in particular the physically and mentally handicapped, but in practice it included those whose protests had excluded them from their professions and who needed material and spiritual support. The church thus took on an intermediary role, relieving the government of a financial burden of welfare and gaining in importance as more and more groups and individuals pursued protest to the point of suffering at the hands of the state. Small groups concerned with peace issues, the environment, and the arbitrary nature of the legal system found common ground in and around the Lutheran Church. Rooms

were made available, contacts were made; slowly a network of opposition was built up, despite continual harassment by the Stasi.

HUMAN RIGHTS

When East Germany signed the Helsinki Accords on Security and Cooperation in Europe in 1975, the final text included sections on human rights. East German citizens subsequently sought

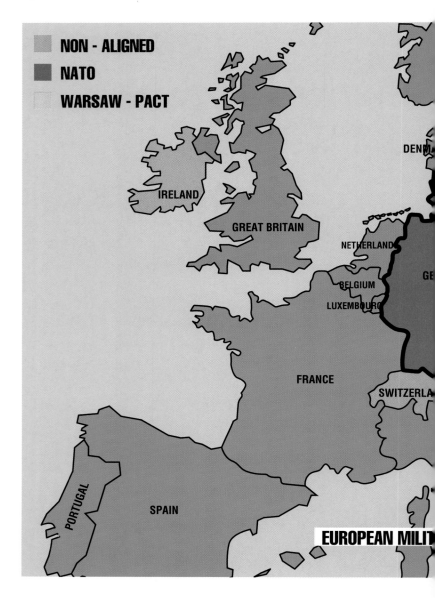

to make their country comply internally with its international obligations. Case followed case with bewildering rapidity, the best known of which concerned the repression that followed protests against the exiling of the popular singer Wolf Biermann in 1976 and the imprisonment of the political critic Rudolf Bahro in 1978.

In the late 1970s the example of Solidarity in Poland spurred protesters in East Germany, but the strict control exercised by the Communist Party over the trade union movement prevented workers from coordinating their efforts. In Lenin's phrase, trade unions were seen as the transmission belt of party orders through the state to the work force. Under sometimes appalling industrial conditions, the workers responded not with fundamental opposition but rather with sullen refusal to exert

LIANCES, 1990

themselves in a production process they perceived as being managed against their interests. The rising of June 1953 and its bloody suppression remained a vivid memory, and it seemed suicidal to repeat the attempt until the situation in the Soviet Union changed. Opposition was concentrated mainly in major cities, especially Berlin and Leipzig, but also

in some smaller university towns and industrial centers such as Erfurt and Jena. Open defiance of the all-embracing state was rare and always swiftly punished. In Jena, for instance, a lone protester was jailed for riding his bicycle through the town with a Solidarity pennant prominent on the handlebars. Apart from a few such flamboyant public acts it was, as one of the leading dissidents of the time so graphically said, as quiet as a graveyard as long as the old regime lasted.

Military rivalry between the Warsaw Pact and NATO set the two Germanys against each other. The growing gulf between the wealth of the West and the material inadequacy of the East reinforced the initial excuse for building the Berlin Wall. The two countries' very different criteria and systems for the distribution of wealth — individualism and free enterprise in the West, government intervention and social priorities in the East — always turned "peaceful coexistence" into a highly charged form of competition. An East German peace activist was subjected to Stasi interrogation for two months at the end of 1983 for merely discussing peace issues privately with a visiting West German politician. The Berlin Wall stood as the lasting symbol of the differences between two German states — regrettable, inhuman, inevitable.

GOOD NEIGHBORLY RELATIONS

While both Germanys established themselves domestically and on the world stage, each was also trying to manage the critical relationship with its neighbor to its own best advantage.

Initially East Germany pursued a policy of encouraging unification of the two states. In the still fluid situation of the 1940s and early 1950s, there was just a chance the socialist model might become dominant. The national anthem of East Germany, written in 1949, speaks of *"Deutschland einzig Vaterland"* — Germany, one Fatherland. But by the end of the 1950s that chance existed no more. The text was changed to omit any reference to a single Germany, and from the 1960s on East Germany stressed the different nature of the socialist state, clearly distinguishing between the single German nation and the two German states. It was a reflex of self-defense.

For West Germany the situation was the reverse. Initially cool to practical measures to encourage unification, in its constitution West Germany nonetheless claimed the right to speak for all Germans, even those in the East "to whom participation was denied" because they were unable to vote on the text submitted for approval by regional parliaments in West Germany. Hence West Germany offered its nationality and passport to any East German who requested it, claiming political authority over all Germans if not over the territory of East Germany. Until the 1970s West Germany

Chancellor Willi Brandt's Ostpolitik *embraced more than improving relations with East Germany. In Warsaw in 1970 he demonstratively knelt to pay homage to the heroes of the Warsaw Ghetto, victims of Nazi barbarity thirty years before.*

refused to recognize diplomatically countries that recognized East Germany, and would not aid Third World nations that had diplomatic relations with its socialist rival.

The Four Powers Agreement on Berlin, which took effect in 1971, reflected the changing relationship between the Soviet Union and the United States. In a growing climate of détente, the Social Democratic chancellor, Willi Brandt, launched a new policy toward the East: *Ostpolitik*, aimed at furthering what Brandt called "good neighborly relations" instead of the hostility of the past. None

of West Germany's basic claims changed, but it stopped aiming its policy at grand international gestures and concentrated instead on practical steps to make life easier for those living in East Germany. It was a policy pursued from a position of strength: Bonn offered generous aid in exchange for East German agreement to make humanitarian gestures and accord limited rights, in particular that of travel abroad.

In this new climate, inter-German contacts, especially trade, grew by leaps and bounds, reaching close to 16 billion Deutsche Marks (DM) at its peak in the mid-1980s. Visits by West Germans across the border to see relatives in East Germany became more common, reaching several million annually at their peak. One-third of West Germans have relatives in the East; two-thirds of East Germans have family in the West. School classes arranged educational visits. Most of the traffic was from West to East, but through this a sense of common German identity was consciously fostered by West Germany's *Ostpolitik*. It was to be a long-term investment.

East Germany was prepared to go along with this in exchange for major short-term financial support. West German payments covered the pensions of East German citizens who settled in the West after retirement age. West Germany paid high fees for services for West Berlin (garbage collection, water supply, improvements to access roads, fees for transit over East German territory). And it supplied generous trade and other credits totaling billions of Deutsche Marks. Starting in 1963 extra payments were made for the early release of political prisoners, accounting for over thirty thousand people by the time the Wall came down.

More than two hundred thousand people fled East Germany between 1961 and 1988. They came mostly via third countries, but some braved the Wall or the inter-German border. Their numbers were a measure of the pent-up desire among East German citizens to travel and experience life in the West. In the same period just under four hundred thousand left the country legally, either as pensioners or after making a case that the authorities could not refuse. Estimates (which cannot be substantiated) suggest that up to a quarter of a million applications to emigrate were pending at any one time in

East Germany. What is certain is that the number actually allowed to go was only a small fraction of those who wanted to leave, but after the establishment of "good neighborly relations" the numbers actually allowed out grew each year.

CHANGING SUPERPOWER RELATIONS

Inter-German relations were inevitably subservient to relations between the superpowers. The spirit of détente, which began with the Four Powers Agreement on Berlin, carried over into the Conference on Security and Cooperation in Europe (CSCE). This culminated in the Helsinki Accords in 1975, which not only confirmed the political borders of postwar Europe, but opened possibilities for economic cooperation and established standards for the respect of human rights in all the countries that signed. These last two sets of issues were vital to the success of inter-German relations and contributed eventually to the collapse of the Communist regime in East Germany.

As diplomatically as possible, financial support from West Germany was linked to improvements in East Germans' living conditions. Above all, the practical conditions under which citizens of the two Germanys could travel between the two countries were constantly improved in response to Bonn's financial support for East Germany. Such linkage became most evident when in 1983 the first one billion DM loan to East Germany coincided with the removal of automatic firing devices on the inter-German border. But there were many lesser examples, such as the expansion of time limits for day trips to East Berlin and the enlargement of categories of West German citizens who could pay reduced visiting fees and visa charges.

The CSCE process alone, however, was not enough to make a fundamental change in the way the Germanys related to each other. For this, an improvement in superpower relations was required, and for some years that was not on the horizon. On the contrary, relations between Moscow and Washington deteriorated, the arms race escalated, and the Soviet Union was cast as the "Evil Empire."

The clash of superpower interests exemplified by the military buildup of the late 1970s had a pro-

found effect in both Germanys. Following NATO's decision in 1979 to negotiate the removal of Soviet SS-20 nuclear missiles and to put its own short-range nuclear weapons in Western Europe, including West Germany, East Germany tried to destabilize its western neighbor through the peace move-

Social problems in West Berlin in the early 1980s brought violent clashes between police and demonstrators sympathizing with squatters who took over unoccupied housing. The protestors developed an alternative life-style that attracted many young people to the city, where they could also avoid the military draft.

ment in the West. Official demonstrations in East Germany raised awareness of peace issues, but spontaneous, non-party involvement was repressed. The emphasis of the public debate was on short-range missiles, for, with a brutal turn of phrase, the

Germans perceived that "the shorter the range, the deader the Germans."

In 1981 one hundred thousand people demonstrated in Bonn, demanding an end to the stationing of NATO'S Cruise and Pershing missiles in Germany. It was the biggest demonstration in the history of West Germany. In the East, the Communist-sponsored Peace Front organized immense rallies against the NATO plans and invited prominent Western peace lobbyists to participate. While these demonstrations did not change policy, they did develop a common understanding and concern for the fragility of peace in both Germanys. And they helped establish a common German interest in an issue that transcended party politics and even the ideological divide. Serious attention came to be paid in both Germanys to the notion of "common security," both in the official structures of the government and ruling party and in the churches and opposition groups. The seriousness of the situation and the fragility of peace at the point where NATO and the Warsaw Pact faced each other over a divided Germany concentrated minds in the search for alternatives to conflict.

Mikhail Gorbachev's accession to power in the Soviet Union in 1985 turned around this deteriorating situation. Within a couple of years it was clear that he was fully in charge and that perestroika, glasnost, and détente were for real. It took some time, but the international implications of this change were, and still are, revolutionary. The world is even now coming to terms with the new relationship between a retreating but reforming Soviet Union and a strained but triumphant United States of America. In the atmosphere of that relationship, the two Germanys are drawing ever closer together.

Germany is special. No other country was divided in two in 1945, with one part on each side of the Iron Curtain. The peaceful revolution in East Germany does not simply mean that another country has turned its back on Communism.

FROM
REVOLUTION TO UNIFICATION

Lenin said, "You can't make an omelette without cracking eggs. You can't make a revolution without spilling blood." The events of 1989 and 1990 in Eastern Europe came close to proving him wrong. Where the revolutions were most thorough, they were least violent, as in East Germany.

EAST GERMANY: A SPECIAL CASE IN EASTERN EUROPE

Germany is special. No other country was divided in two in 1945, with one part on each side of the Iron Curtain. The peaceful revolution in East Germany does not simply mean that another country has turned its back on Communism. That is true of Poland, of Czechoslovakia, of Hungary, to a lesser degree even of Bulgaria and Romania. But in Germany it means more than that. It means that the German Communist experiment has failed and that the German capitalist system has won the struggle for the moral allegiance of all the people. Germany as a whole will be bigger and stronger as a result of the East German revolution on West German principles.

The contest between the two systems was more obvious in Germany than elsewhere. Observers could compare West and East, capitalist and Communist, democratic and totalitarian across one nation divided into two states. A short walk from one side of the Berlin Wall to the other showed the contrast at its most stark.

Germany was the propaganda battleground, and it was also the potential armed battleground. The Cold War was a time of global tension, but the superpowers were involved in Germany in greater force than anywhere else on earth. There the armies of the Western Allies and the Soviet Union were in close range; NATO and the Warsaw Pact maneuvered within sight of the barbed-wire divide that ran the length of the country. It was clear for all to see that change in Germany depended on changes in relations between the two blocs, and more particularly between the United States and the Soviet Union.

In 1985 those relations began to improve dramatically. The election of Mikhail Gorbachev as secretary-general of the Soviet Communist Party was the key to that change. But he was elected by a margin of only one vote in the Politburo, after his two predecessors had died within barely a year. Gorbachev inherited a party confused and deeply divided about how to cope with a rapidly deteriorating economy. Theoretically the most powerful man in the Soviet Union, he still needed two years to establish himself fully as undisputed leader. He reached that point in 1987, when he ousted Andrei Gromyko, the long-serving and influential former foreign minister, from the post of president of the Supreme Soviet.

By then the direction of the changes Gorbachev wanted — glasnost (openness) and perestroika (economic reform) — was obvious, and their speed was accelerating. For the United States and its allies these changes were reflected in important disarmament agreements, which the West saw both as a relief and a new challenge. But for the countries of Eastern Europe, held tightly within the Soviet Union's traditional sphere of influence, it was a revolution. Upon his return from a visit to Washington, Gorbachev announced the end of the Brezhnev Doctrine, the policy used to justify Soviet intervention in internal affairs within the Eastern bloc. From then on, he declared, it would be the "Sinatra" Doctrine: each country could do it "My Way." It was a signal that East European reformers hardly dared believe could be true.

The Hungarians were the first to test the water. In September 1987 Imre Pozsgay, the leading Hungarian reformer, called for a new constitution to guarantee freedom of expression. The following May the aging leader, Janos Kadar, who had been

Seven leaders of Warsaw Pact states in 1987. Now only two remain: Gorbachev and Jaruzelski. Gone are Husak from Czechoslovakia, Shivkov from Bulgaria, Honecker from East Germany, Ceaucescu from Romania and Kadar from Hungary. And in Poland General Jaruzelski shares power with Prime Minister Mazowiecki (right) while Lech Walesa (left) heads the anti-Communist movement, Solidarity.

installed by the Russians when they put down the Hungarian revolution in 1956, resigned as Communist Party leader. In January 1989 the leaders of the 1956 revolution were rehabilitated and given a public funeral with full honor. The following month the Hungarian Communist Party formally accepted the need for a multiparty democracy, renouncing its monopoly on power. In May 1989

the foreign ministers of Hungary and Austria ceremonially cut the barbed-wire fence that marked the border between their countries. It was the first rip in the Iron Curtain.

Changes had begun in Poland even earlier, but they were initially put down with force. The free trade union movement Solidarity kept up a running battle with the Communist Party from its beginnings in Gdansk in 1980, even though a declaration of martial law in December 1981 put most of the Solidarity leaders behind bars. General Wojciech Jaruzelski bought more time for his Communist regime while waiting for Soviet reforms to increase Poland's political room to maneuver. In November 1987 he put limited proposals for reform to a referendum but they were rejected. It was clear that the country wanted more fundamental freedoms. The first multiparty elections, in June 1989, were won overwhelmingly by Solidarity candidates. By August the Polish parliament had endorsed Tadeusz Mazowiecki as the first non-Communist prime minister of a country in the Soviet bloc.

In Bulgaria the Communist leader, Todor Zhivkov, initially supported Gorbachev's aims of glasnost and perestroika, until he realized they were more than mere propaganda slogans. Openness and restructuring in a country like Bulgaria, misruled for more than forty years and suffering economic hardship, environmental pollution, and ethnic conflict, could only mean the end of the Communist monopoly on power.

In October 1989, Petar Mladenov, Zhivkov's longtime foreign minister, precipitated a government crisis as protestors used an international human rights conference in the Bulgarian capital to point up the country's appalling record on that issue. Gorbachev and Mladenov had been students together in Moscow in the early 1960s, and with Soviet support Mladenov ousted Zhivkov on the very day the Berlin Wall was opened. A month later the Communist Party renounced its monopoly on power and agreed to take part in free elections the following year.

Such developments, especially those in Hungary and Poland, were not lost on the East Germans. Voice of America, Radio Free Europe, Radio Liberty, Deutsche Welle, and the BBC kept listeners up to date, and for most of the country West German television provided visible evidence of the change going on around them. But while the cutting of the wire fence that separated Hungary from Austria gave them hope that some day the wall and the wire that divided Germany would also come down, at home all they saw was a stubborn refusal to reform — a situation that became increasingly unbearable.

EAST GERMANY: RHETORIC AND REALITY

The East German leadership, as so often in the Communist world, was a gerontocracy, a government of old men. Erich Honecker, the party leader, was born in 1912. So was Kurt Hager, the ideology chief. Erich Mielke, head of security, was born in 1907. They were committed Communists. They had suffered under the Nazis and had come to Berlin behind the Red Army in 1945 with proud ideals of social progress, to set up the first socialist state in Germany. But they had failed to recruit and prepare successors with an equal commitment. Many of the next generation were associated with the ruling party essentially because it was the necessary gateway to advancement. As the first generation of politicians aged, so enthusiasm and idealism turned to careerism and even cynicism.

Not that the SED, the East German Communist Party, was at a loss for recruits. Whether for noble motives or base, more than two and a half million people were members. Membership was seen as a privilege bringing obligation (in principle) and advantages (in practice), which ranged from the small services that party members rendered each other locally to the major benefits enjoyed by the leadership. The *nomenklatura*, those with positions who benefited from the regime in a major way, may well have been as large as half a million. Their support was what bolstered the leadership.

As long as Soviet policy remained as it had been for more than a generation, the East German leadership was secure. Nearly four hundred thousand Soviet troops were stationed in East Germany and the Soviet leaders had shown in the workers' rising of 1953 that they were prepared to use them. On top of that the leadership deployed an extensive

The past and the privileged: Erich Honecker (top left) and his chosen successor, Egon Krenz (top right), being interviewed by RIAS TV; Markus Wolf (mid-left), spymaster of East Germany, whose successful penetration of West Germany forced Chancellor Brandt to resign; and Kurt Hager (mid-right), aging ideology chief and scourge of the intellectuals. Luxury villas, such as those in Wandlitz, and access to hard currency shops were among the privileges of the nomenclatura, *the leaders of the regime, that were denied to the less privileged in this classless society.*

and efficient system of internal security to ensure that dissent was nipped in the bud. An obedient East Germany was Moscow's loyal ally. For many, that was the only imaginable East Germany.

Under this apparently smooth surface there was widespread dissatisfaction among East German people with the conditions in which they lived. TV and radio gave them not only news of political developments in the outside world but images of a lifestyle in the West beyond their wildest dreams. Though very few of them were allowed to travel to see for themselves, West German visitors brought the reality of a richer material society in the cars they drove, the clothes they wore, the presents they bestowed. Many East German citizens received subsidies from their richer relatives in the West. With hard currency from the West, they could buy Western goods in special government-run shops. For those who had the hard currency, it was an ambiguous advantage, a limited improvement to their living standards, which left them hungry for more. For those without access to hard currency, it simply bred envy of others and anger with the system.

East Germany as a state also became dependent on its rich neighbor. Grants and loans worth millions of Deutsche Marks maintained the creditworthiness of East Germany on international markets and helped pay for its imports of vital West German industrial goods. Some of the biggest loans topped $500 million. The public rhetoric of the leadership in the East became increasingly hypocritical, criticizing the failings of its capitalist Western sibling while receiving the financial surplus that system generated. It was a gross example of the deterioration of the ideals of the socialist state. Moral corruption increasingly divided reality from the language used to describe it. The Berlin Wall, for instance, was officially called an "anti-fascist defensive rampart." The regime had lost whatever initial legitimacy it claimed. The leaders knew — and as the 1970s passed more and more of the people knew — that without Soviet support the regime would fall.

Criticism of the leadership's hypocrisy and duplicity had come as much from idealistic Communists bent on reform from within the system as from opponents of the system wanting to bring it

down. In 1968, for criticizing East Germany's decision to send troops to help the Soviets suppress the Prague Spring, a leading Communist, Robert Havermann, had been dismissed from his government position and excluded from the party. He was held in internal exile under permanent police supervision until he died in 1982. Havermann's analysis of what was wrong with "real existing socialism" laid the foundation for much of the idealistic internal criticism that sparked off the peaceful revolution twenty years later.

The satirical songs of ballad singer Wolf Biermann, East Germany's intellectual version of Bob Dylan, made him a popular figure in East Germany in the 1970s. When he was sent into exile in 1976 for offending the leaders' idea of ideological purity, it brought a wave of protest from artists and intellectuals. In the resulting crackdown, hundreds lost their jobs or were refused permission to publish, exhibit, or perform. Other intellectuals read the score and went down the road of self-censorship, avoiding controversy. German artists knew this experience from the Nazi years and called it "inner emigration." East German arts and letters suffered as a result, and opposition forces gained among the intelligentsia.

In 1980 a middle-ranking civil servant, Rudolf Bahro, was imprisoned for publishing in the West his critical appraisal of East German government and society. As a result, more of the young intelligentsia, especially academics and bureaucrats, grew disillusioned with the intolerance and inflexibility of the aging leadership.

Both the number and the size of small opposition groups slowly grew during the 1980s, largely under the protection of the Lutheran Church. But their open gestures of protest were few. Since the groups were not coordinated, they posed no practical challenge to the regime. Stasi informers kept the authorities up to date on their brave but minor acts of defiance.

In January 1988, however, an official demonstration to mark the anniversary of the assassination of Rosa Luxemburg, one of the founding figures of German Communism, served as the occasion for a more serious public challenge. A group of dissidents joined the official march and unfurled a banner with a slogan that had not been approved in advance by the authorities: "Freedom is always the freedom for others to disagree" — a quotation from Luxemburg herself. Police intervened brutally and arrested close to a hundred protesters, but not before Western journalists had witnessed the scene. The authorities were appalled that a demonstration called to celebrate one of the regime's saints should have been perverted to serve the opposition's ends. Sentences of prison or temporary exile were quickly passed on the leaders, but the opposition was now clearly out in the open.

In September 1988 Erich Honecker visited Moscow and was obliged to declare support for Mikhail Gorbachev's policy for renewing Soviet society. The irony of Honecker's public support for Gorbachev's actions in the Soviet Union and his continued repression of dissent at home was not lost on the East German populace. Dissident groups began to broaden their demands for a more responsive and popular form of government. To head off opposition, local elections were organized in May 1989 after a lapse of many years, and candidates not associated with the Communist Party were allowed to run. But official figures still gave 98.85 percent of the vote to the officially approved parties led by the SED. Church and opposition groups voiced widespread public disgust with the system and condemned the elections as rigged.

Since the division of Germany the East German government had given orders to shoot would-be escapees, both at the Wall and at the border between the two countries. Despite growing détente between the superpowers, that order was not rescinded. In early 1989, border guards shot and killed an East German trying to escape over the Wall. A few weeks later guards shot and wounded two other would-be refugees. It was brutal and conclusive proof that the government had no trust in its own people. The gulf between the people and the party that ran the government grew ever wider.

In June 1989 the Communist Party's official newspaper, *Neues Deutschland*, defended the Chinese authorities' massacre of students on Tiananmen Square in Beijing. The East German parliament unanimously endorsed the party line, praising the "restoration of order and security by the use of armed force." Egon Krenz, Honecker's chosen successor, was visiting China at the time and personally endorsed the crackdown. In East Germany it was clear that even if Honecker were to step down, the party line would not change.

The February 1988 official demonstration in East Berlin in honor of Rosa Luxembourg and Karl Liebknecht, where dissidents mounted their biggest challenge yet to the Communist system. In June 1989 the Foreign Ministers of Hungary and Austria, Gyula Horn and Alois Mock, started to dismantle the Iron Curtain along their common border.

ESCAPE, REFORM, OR REVOLUTION

Events elsewhere in Eastern Europe were rapidly leaving East Germany isolated. The Hungarian reformist regime's decision to loosen its strict control on the border to Austria in May 1989 had been the first opening of the Iron Curtain. To those who could read the writing on the wall, it spelled the beginning of the end of the hard-line regimes of Eastern Europe.

Bärbel Bohley, dissident artist and "Mother of the Revolution," repeatedly arrested, imprisoned, and exiled. She co-founded with Jens Reich and Rolf Hendrich the reform group New Forum, meeting here in the Gethsemane Church in East Berlin. New Forum articulated environmental and peace concerns in a climate of intellectual freedom while seeking a dialogue with the authorities to restore trust between government and the people.

In July and early August, the West received reports of East German citizens seeking asylum in West German embassies in Budapest and Prague. Both Hungary and Czechoslovakia had agreements with East Germany requiring them to return any would-be refugees caught on their territory. Back home they would be imprisoned. Thus those seeking asylum were effectively confined to the embassies. As the numbers swelled to hundreds, the

embassies had to close. In mid-August close to nine hundred East German citizens used the confusion of a popular "pan-European picnic" in western Hungary to slip over the open border with Austria to freedom. It was the beginning of the mass flight of refugees from East Germany. Every successful escape encouraged those left behind.

Celebrations for the fortieth anniversary of the founding of the country were being planned for October; bad publicity was the last thing the East German government wanted. But on September 11, 1989, the Hungarian government publicly denounced its agreement with East Germany and officially opened its border with Austria. Within three days more than fifteen thousand East German citizens used that route to flee to the West. In West German embassies in Prague and Warsaw, thousands more were waiting for their chance, and the numbers were growing daily. Finally, under pressure from West Germany, Poland, and Czechoslovakia, East Germany agreed to let the refugees out. They had to travel in special trains across East German territory to maintain the fiction that they were not "escaping" but being "sent into exile." As the trains passed through the country, thousands more would-be refugees tried to storm them to get free passage to the West. In Dresden more than three thousand fought with police at the station. Forty years of socialism had not persuaded them to stay and build their future in East Germany.

Inside East Germany the disparate opposition groups gained confidence. In the shadow of the wave of refugees leaving the country in September, thirty representatives from all over East Germany met in Robert Havermann's former home in Grünheide to found a critical movement, "New Forum." They were mostly intellectuals — prominent among them a painter, a biologist, a lawyer, a physicist, and a theologian — and several of them had suffered at the hands of the Stasi. The founders wanted to reform the system to secure a pluralist democracy but retain what they saw as progressive elements of socialism. New Forum was to be a platform for honest debate, to restore trust between the people and their government.

The founders were overwhelmed by the countrywide response to their appeal. Local versions of

New Forum sprang up in many towns; the network came together. Their initiative even stirred up opposition in some of the parties that traditionally followed the Communist lead. The situation was obviously serious. Yet it was right before the fortieth anniversary celebrations, so the government shrank from clamping down on dissent for fear of international reaction.

The official celebrations in October 1989 brought Mikhail Gorbachev to East Berlin. The crowds appealed directly to him, shouting: "Gorby, help us!" The East German leaders were not pleased, but in the situation they could do nothing but grin and bear it. Gorbachev made the situation worse for them when he publicly declared, "History will pass by those who do not change." It was a signal to the *nomenklatura* that Erich Honecker was no longer the man to lead the party. Within a fortnight he had retired "for health reasons," to be replaced by Egon Krenz.

The new leader lasted just over six weeks. He was doomed from the start. The party was still in two minds about how to cope with open dissent. Hard-liners close to Krenz wanted to put it down with force. Reformers wanted dialogue, and even considered sharing power. In the end concessions were made. Demonstrations were permitted outside party control. These grew to enormous size, bringing hundreds of thousands regularly onto the streets, particularly in Leipzig. *"Wir sind das Volk"* (We are the people), they chanted, and later, *"Wir sind* ein *Volk"* (We are *one* people). The implications for reunification were obvious.

The government was forced to relax travel restrictions to the West and began to concede other reforms. Some cosmetic changes were approved, among them a revision of the words of the national anthem to refer to a "single Fatherland" again. But these changes were not enough to restore faith in the party leadership.

Soon after Krenz assumed power a wave of revelations about corruption swept away senior figures both in the party and in government. In Communist countries the party apparatus is officially separate from the government, but as the "vanguard of the proletariat" it effectively controls the state and dictates policy to government. The party Politburo is the real focus of power; government

ministries carry out its will. Exposure of corruption and abuse of power brought down several key figures of the old guard of the party close to the former leader, including his wife, Margot Honecker, who had been minister of education for many years. As the party was weakened by revelations of corruption, it became more and more preoccupied with internal reform in the interests of sheer survival. And as the party became less dominant, so the government gained some margin to act more independently, though it lacked any tradition of independence.

Weakness at the top allowed power to slip to the people. On November 4 more than a million people demonstrated in East Berlin for freedom

1989 saw the biggest demonstrations since the East German rising of June 1953. Peaceful demonstrations in major cities — like the seventy thousand people here on the streets of Leipzig in October — first demanded freedom to travel, then other political rights. By the end of November the crowds were openly calling for unification with West Germany. 1989 saw the biggest demonstrations since the East German rising of June 1953.

and free elections. Three days later the entire government resigned. The day after that the whole Politburo followed. It was the point of crisis in the revolution. The leadership failed to decide either to suppress the popular movement by force or to accede to its fundamental demands. Indecision cost the party its power.

Opinions continued divided, and Egon Krenz clung to his position at the head of a smaller Politburo. But the reformers in the party gained the majority and set in train changes designed to gain time for the Communists to reform and reassert their leading role. High on their list of changes was the opening of the Berlin Wall, the ultimate gesture designed to stop mass migration to the West. With the wall open and freedom of travel to and fro assured, argued the reformers, there would be less incentive for the disgruntled populace to flee for good from East Germany. It was a cold calculation presented as a grand gesture, and it caught the imagination of the world.

It is a historical irony that the wall was built in 1961 to stop East Germans from moving to the West, and it was pulled down in 1989 for the same reason. It was a last gamble by the Communist authorities. They offered their discontented population easier access to the West in the desperate hope that freedom to travel would reconcile the people to living in the materially and spiritually impoverished East. And all the while, behind this seemingly humane gesture, hard-liners in the government and party were preparing to break up mass demonstrations by force and planning internment camps for the ringleaders of the opposition.

The new government installed in early November was headed by Hans Modrow, a reform-minded Communist Party leader from Dresden. He had fallen out with Honecker's leadership several years before and came to government with some claim to moral support even outside the SED. Widely regarded as incorrupt, he concentrated his efforts on restoring the credibility of the government, drawing in expertise from beyond the closed circle of the party faithful and their traditional allies.

While Modrow was widening the appeal of the government, Krenz was waging a losing battle for credibility inside the Communist Party. Reforms had brought some new faces to the top, but the self-confidence of rank and file members was shattered by the extent of the popular opposition. Hundreds of thousands of members handed in their party cards. Honest and idealistic Communists knew the reform had to go much deeper. The Communist Party would have to renounce its claim to lead society in the name of the working class, and become a political party like any other in a pluralist, democratic society. Members demonstrated outside party headquarters in Berlin, demanding fun-

damental reform. The East German parliament, the Volkskammer, officially removed from the constitution the party's claim to the leading role in society. On December 6, Egon Krenz resigned from the leadership of a Communist Party in a state of collapse.

The day after Krenz's fall, the Lutheran Church in East Germany, encouraged by Modrow, invited all political groups to roundtable talks with the government. The years of repression had failed, and the attempt to buy time with concessions had

Outside the secret police (Stasi) headquarters in numerous towns, East Germans lit candles as memorials to those arrested, imprisoned, or exiled for their opposition to the Communist state. Despite the Stasi's files on more than four million citizens and an extensive network of informers, knowledge that the Soviet army would not back them made the secret police impotent against the peoples' massive, persistent, non-violent protests.

failed. Now the search was on in earnest for consensus in a shattered society. The Communists and the five parties associated with them in government met with seven opposition groups, prominent among them New Forum and the recently founded Social Democratic Party.

The roundtable agreed at its first session to hold free elections in May 1990. It went on to meet weekly and suggest major changes to the way society was run, including a social charter to protect citizens' rights, a new constitution to limit the power of government over the individual, and the abolition of the secret police, the Stasi. Krenz's successor as party leader, Gregor Gysi, agreed to all these points; he could not do otherwise since members were leaving the party in thousands and those who stayed envisaged a renewed and regenerated Communist Party, not the sham that had ruled the country for forty years.

ECONOMICS AND ELECTIONS

As the old parties reformed and new parties were established, the life-and-death struggle of the East German economy was being played out at governmental level, in particular with the government in Bonn. In the middle of November the perceptive Social Democratic mayor of West Berlin, Walter Momper, analyzed the problem accurately. In the huge demonstrations so far, Momper argued, no group in East Germany had openly called for unification as the goal of the peaceful revolution. "The question is, however, will leading circles on our side of the Wall give the democratic revolution in East Germany a chance, or will they pursue their secret aim of simply letting East Germany collapse under the weight of its economic difficulties? Will we really help a new East Germany or are our own ideology and national interest stronger? Are we speculating that East Germany will sell itself to the highest bidder? That their currency will go through the floor? Right now that is the key question that divides us in Germany."

At the end of November 1989, Chancellor Helmut Kohl, leader of the Christian Democrat-led Bonn government, announced an ambitious ten-point program for German unification. He did not consult his Western allies beforehand and his plans for speedy union shocked many cautious observers. But Kohl saw the opportunity that West German economic strength gave him and he seized it with both hands. The moment called for action and he decided he was the leader best placed to decide the course of events.

Kohl spoke frequently by phone with Hans Modrow in East Berlin. Modrow visited Bonn later in search of practical, and sizable, economic aid. He

West German Chancellor Kohl, the central actor in the German drama, with East German Prime Minister Modrow (top) and with the Soviet President (middle) when Gorbachev visited Bonn in June 1989. Nine months later the Germans wrote "Gorby" their thank you letter on the western side of the broken Berlin Wall.

received warm words of moral encouragement but only a few small practical gestures to further the reforms he was introducing into the system. The West German government was not interested in bolstering a dying Communist regime, even when Modrow appointed leading opposition figures from the roundtable to ministerial posts. Bonn's concern was ensuring that the planned elections in East Germany returned a solid majority in favor of unification, which meant opening up East Germany to West German economic interests.

East Germans used to wait up to ten years for delivery of a new two-stroke Trabant — nicknamed "Trabi" — despite its noise and high pollution. Second-hand they cost more than new, since there was no wait for delivery. Now production has stopped and Trabis finish up in garbage dumps.

Faced with an increasingly hopeless economic situation, scores of thousands of East German citizens continued to flee to the West. As the new parties jockeyed for position in East Germany, the situation grew increasingly untenable. With no adequate sources of capital investment, the Modrow government brought the elections forward from May to March 1990.

Migration to West Germany was over two hundred fifty thousand in 1989 alone. It was causing social tension in the West as newcomers took jobs and housing from local citizens. Some towns, notably Bremen, indicated they could not take more East German refugees. Their resources were overstretched. Occasional acts of violence — particularly against the ubiquitous Trabant, the small, noisy car driven by many who came West — reminded the refugees of the tensions just below the surface.

The situation was made worse in some big towns, like West Berlin, by thousands of East Germans ("*Ossis*") visiting and buying whatever they could not get in the East. Border and customs controls broke down. Soon a range of Western goods could be seen on roadside stalls in the East, being bought by a populace eager to spend its Eastern marks before they dropped in value. The exchange rate between Deutsche Mark and Ost Mark (OM) became a speculator's paradise, falling as low as 20 to 1. West Germany stepped in to stabilize the currency. Kohl's promise of a 1-to-1 exchange rate at the official level became one of the strongest cards to be played by the Bonn government in the election campaign.

East Germany's first free elections were dominated by major West German politicians. Willi Brandt, former chancellor and architect of *Ostpolitik*, spoke to huge crowds on behalf of the newly founded Social Democratic Party of East Germany. Hans-Dietrich Genscher, West Germany's foreign minister, campaigned for the Free Democrat/Liberal alliance. Chancellor Kohl was enthusiastically received, especially in the southern, industrial areas of East Germany, when he toured for the Conservative Alliance, led by the Christian Democrats. The campaign at times looked like an extension of West German politics. Parties such as New Forum, which had no counterpart in the West, were starved of money and manpower while the Christian Democrats, the Social Democrats, and the Free Democrats sent money and staff to back up their political allies' campaigns in the East.

In all, twenty-four parties contested four hundred seats. The Conservative Alliance won one hundred and ninety-three, just short of an absolute majority. The Social Democrats won eighty-seven, the reformed Communist Party sixty-five, and the Liberals twenty-one. New Forum, linked with Democracy Now and the International League for Human Rights in a grouping called Bündnis 90, won only twelve seats. The Farmers' Party won

Elections brought West German politicians into East Germany to campaign. Here Willi Brandt electioneers at a rally in Greifswald. The Conservative Alliance won just short of an absolute majority, but their leader, Lothar de Maizière (top), had to rely on the Social Democrats in a coalition to have enough votes in Parliament to pass the constitutional changes needed for unification.

nine and the Greens eight, and five other seats were shared by smaller parties.

The 93 percent turnout was less of a surprise than the strength of the Conservative Alliance. The alliance's policy of speedy unification was strongly endorsed by East German voters; in some regions they won 60 percent or more of the vote. The Social Democrats did badly with their policy of maintaining two Germanys for a while and negotiating unification over a longer period. The people were impatient: they wanted Western standards of living and Western freedoms as soon as possible.

After some initial hesitations even the Social Democrats joined with the conservatives to form a grand coalition in the new parliament. The new government was thus assured of a two-thirds majority and hence the possibility of altering the East German constitution to allow union with West Germany. As one politician put it, "This government has a mandate to dissolve the state."

The new government of East Germany was headed by Lothar de Maizière as Christian Democratic prime minister, with a leading Social Democrat, Markus Meckel, as foreign minister. East German government leaders negotiated with West Germany to try to maintain some of the social rights and benefits acquired under the old regime (for instance, housing benefits and guaranteed employment) and to arrange adequate transitional measures, especially concerning compensation to East Germans for expropriated property now being reclaimed by West Germans. But East Germany was negotiating from a position of economic weakness. Informed estimates suggested that one East German factory in five would close immediately, three in five might survive if restructured with new capital, and only one in five was viable in its present form. Unemployment was expected to reach anything between 20 percent and 40 percent of the work force within a year. The only remedies in sight were emigration to the West, foreign investment, or unemployment subsidies. East Germany had all of the problems and none of the solutions.

When local elections were held in East Germany in May 1990, the overwhelming power of West Germany was again felt strongly. Just two days before the vote, Chancellor Kohl confirmed there would be a 1-for-1 exchange rate in the Treaty

There were celebrations on the streets on 1 July 1990 when Deutsche Marks replaced Ost Marks in currency union — the first step toward political union. At last East Germans had hard currency to buy quality goods from the West. Barrow loads of useless Ost Marks were wheeled away to be destroyed.

on Monetary, Economic and Social Union then under negotiation. The same day the "two-plus-four" talks began in Bonn, between the two Germanys and the four World War II Allies, on the future of what everyone assumed would soon be a united Germany.

The local elections still showed the Conservative Alliance as the strongest party, with 37 percent. The Social Democrats and other left-of-center parties made only minor gains. The poll largely confirmed the general election of March and reinforced the move toward unity.

The generous agreement on monetary union at a 1-for-1 rate assured East Germans that from July 1990 wages and pensions would be paid in Deutsche Marks, and pensions would be brought up to the more favorable West German proportion of the final year's salary. Personal savings of up to 4,000 OM would be exchanged at parity, with amounts above that exchanged at a rate of 2 OM for 1 DM.

The treaty dealing with monetary union regulates many problems, including settlement of East Germany's more than 50 billion marks — formerly OM, now DM — of government debt. A special fund of nearly 100 billion DM is to aid new government investment and pay the social costs of bringing East Germany into the world market

The end of the division of Berlin and the beginning of the unification of Germany. Redundant guards on the Eastern side watch young West Berliners on top of of the Wall with the old Reichstag (Parliament) building in the background, or sit disconsolently in their jeep while tourists gape through holes in the steel and concrete. Father Christmases with the Brandenburg Gate behind them entertain a crowd. "Trabis" are welcomed by clapping westerners as they cross the Gliericke Bridge, where during the Cold War spy exchanges took place under heavy guard. For weeks after the Wall was opened the streets of West Berlin were crowded with "Ossis" just visiting, enjoying their freedom to travel. Meanwhile work went on day and night to remove the hated symbol of Germany's division.

It is a historical irony that the wall was built in 1961 to stop East Germans from moving to the West — and that it was pulled down in 1989 for the same reason.

economy. But many other issues remain unsolved. West Germany will pay a price in extra inflation to absorb the economic and monetary problems of East Germany, and it has no guarantee that the generous terms of the deal will keep East Germans from migrating West in search of better-paid jobs. Wage levels in the East are bound to rise as productivity rises, but they start at little more than half of West German levels. East Germans are being asked to work harder and accept some years more of austerity and rising unemployment in exchange for low wages (albeit in hard currency) and the freedom to travel just like West Germans.

But it is being made very clear to them that they are no longer encouraged to move to West Germany. "Welcome grants" and subsidized housing are no longer offered. The prospect of working and living in the East under revised conditions is meant to take away the desire to go West to seek a new start with high wages but also high risks and high costs, especially for travel, housing and food. However, prices for these basic goods, heavily subsidized in the old East Germany, are now rising to Western levels there as the economy becomes market-oriented, though previously exorbitantly priced "luxuries," from television sets to refrigerators, are considerably cheaper than before.

THE INTERNATIONAL DIMENSION

The international dimension of German unification draws in many players beyond West Germany and East Germany. The wartime Allies, neighboring countries, and the European Community all have an interest in ensuring that the solution does not destabilize Europe. Old memories die hard, and in the case of Germany, old memories are bad memories of aggression and war. The Soviet Union suggested even before events in East Germany took such a dramatic turn that the Helsinki Conference on Security and Cooperation in Europe be used as the framework to settle pending issues and new ones. At the CSCE summit scheduled for November 19, 1990 in Paris, the implications of German unification for the European continent will undoubtedly be discussed.

The thirty-five-member CSCE, comprising representatives of the United States, Canada, the Soviet Union, and all European countries except Albania, is one body which will bind a united Germany to wider European and international interests. The conference's political, economic, and human rights concerns are the concerns of all the participants. Economically a united Germany will be part of the West, bound into the European Community; indeed, it will be the largest and richest EC member. Militarily the scene is changing fast; the old confrontation between a Western NATO and an Eastern Warsaw Pact is being replaced by cooperation in pursuit of common security interests. "Good neighborly relations," once the key to improving contacts between the two Germanys, are now the key to relations across the continent. If there is to be a "common European home," as Mikhail Gorbachev proposed, then all those living in it and close to it should have their say in how it is to be built and run.

Agreement in the "two-plus-four" discussions on key security issues was vital before the two parts of Germany could proceed with formal unification and common elections. Both the German states and the Allies sought agreement quickly, to ensure as predictable an evolution in Europe as possible. Although it was a hard message to sell to domestic opinion in the Soviet Union, a united Germany within NATO is preferable to an uncertain and neutral Germany belonging to no military alliance. To get the Soviet Union to accept such a solution, NATO transformed its alliance and revised its forward defense strategy, as proclaimed in its London Declaration of July 1990. This placed NATO's future relations with what remains of the Warsaw Pact on a positive rather than an antagonistic footing.

Progress was rapid. The "two-plus-four" Treaty on the Final Settlement with Respect to Germany was signed in Moscow on September 12, paving the way for German unification and preparing Germany's return to full sovereignty. The Soviet Union conceded the right for a united Germany to belong to the NATO alliance while the two Germanys declared that their present borders are final, renouncing all claims to former German land in Poland. Soviet troops are to be repatriated from East Germany by the end of 1994, with West Germany paying 12 billion DM to meet the cost. The

Germanys also agreed to cut their total troops to 370,000 before the Soviet pullout is completed. To further reassure Soviet anxiety at unification, the Western Allies agreed that East German territory will not be used to station or deploy non-German NATO forces or nuclear-capable missile launchers. In addition, the two Germanys declared that their unified state will renounce the possession or use of nuclear, biological, and chemical weapons.

Plenty of other unfinished business remained in relations between the two German states before unification could become a legal and political reality. Issues such as compatibility between the two legal systems required a second treaty, the Treaty on Political Union, to enlarge upon the Treaty on Monetary, Economic and Social Union. It will encompass financial redistribution from the richer West to the poorer Eastern regions, and changes in the structure and function of the courts, as well as key areas of social legislation such as women's rights, including abortion, where the liberal approach of East German legislation is at variance with conservative West German practice.

The East German government is to recreate the regional structure of *Länder* or states, reviving those old regions dissolved by the Nazi regime — Brandenburg, Saxony, Saxony-Anhalt, Thuringia, and Mecklenburg. Political parties in the *Länder* have to organize and select candidates, run elections, and form regional governments. This is essential, as the mechanism for formal unification requires each of the five *Länder* to apply individually to join West Germany. Article 23 of the West German constitution declares that additional *Länder* may join the country, not that East Germany as an entity can apply to join.

Only the most confident and optimistic of those in favor of speedy unification thought all of this could be achieved by the end of 1990 — but they were right. The "two-plus-four" treaty comes into effect October 3. Voting in the five *Länder* takes place on October 14. Joint elections for the new, unified German parliament are set for December 2, 1990.

The Social Democrats, junior partners in the East Berlin government, were initially reluctant to see the pace of unification forced. They worried about the economic cost to East German voters, especially rapidly rising unemployment. The conservatives, partly under pressure from Bonn, wanted to speed up the process, sensing victory if all-German elections were held before the worst economic effects were felt. Ultimately, however, the Social Democrats pushed for even earlier unification than the conservatives wanted. In August 1990 these differences came to a head. Prime Minister de Maizière dismissed four Social Democratic ministers, their party quit the government en bloc, and the conservatives lost the parliamentary majority they needed for a constitutional amendment. Faced with the rapid deterioration of the East German economy, however, the deputies finally voted overwhelmingly for early unification.

Even if disputes upset the election timetable, in the broad sweep of history the revolution in East Germany has taken place with incredible speed. Little more than six months elapsed between the first wave of refugees fleeing through the rip in the Iron Curtain in late summer 1989 and the first free elections in East Germany in March 1990. In less than a year after the Berlin wall was opened, all the necessary legislative and treaty changes leading to unification were completed.

Popular resentment pressured the morally corrupt East German leadership to reforms that were never enough because they were never fundamental. Even the decision to open the Berlin Wall was made in order to keep more of an unwilling populace in a country they wished to leave. T.S. Eliot, in his play *Murder in the Cathedral*, underlined the inherent moral problem of government in such a dilemma: his hero avoided the "last and worst treason," which was "to do the right deed for the wrong reason." Opening the Berlin Wall was the Communists' last and worst treason. East German Communism collapsed under the weight of its own moral degradation. To achieve ends nobody believed in any longer, it resorted to methods nobody could justify. It was swept away by mass defections, mass demonstrations, and a massive popular vote of no confidence as soon as free and fair elections were possible.

KEY DATES IN GERMAN HISTORY

AD 9	Defeat of Roman legions in Teutoburg Forest.
754	Death of St. Boniface.
800	Charlemagne crowned emperor.
1517	Martin Luther's 95 theses at Wittenberg.
1618-1648	Thirty Years War, ended by Peace of Westphalia.
1740	Frederick the Great becomes king of Prussia and seizes Silesia.
1792	French revolutionary wars.
1793	Second partition of Poland.
1795	Third partition of Poland. German states in varying alliances with and against France.
1806	Napoleon forms Confederation of the Rhine; dissolution of Holy Roman Empire of the German Nation.
1813/1815	Napoleon defeated at Leipzig (Battle of the Nations) and Waterloo.
1815	German Confederation founded by victorious powers at Conference of Vienna. Constitutional unrest following successful French revolution.
1830	Beginning of *Zollverein* (customs union).
1834	First German railway, Nuremberg to Fürth.
1835	Deep coal mining in Ruhr begins.
1837	Revolutionary disturbances in Europe; Marx and
1848	Engels issue Communist Manifesto; German National Assembly at Frankfurt.
1862	Otto von Bismarck appointed minister-president of Prussia.
1864	Prussian-Austrian war against Denmark over Schleswig-Holstein.
1866	Seven Weeks War; Austria defeated by Prussia.
1867	North German Confederation, dominated by Prussia.
1870	Napoleon III defeated at Sedan in Franco-Prussian War.
1871	German Empire proclaimed at Versailles.
1888	Accession of William II as German emperor.
1890	Bismarck dismissed.
1904	Entente Cordiale between Britain and France.
1914	Outbreak of World War I.
1917	United States enters war. Bolshevik revolution in Russia.
1918	Treaty of Brest-Litovsk with Soviet Union. Armistice with Western Powers. Emperor William II abdicates.
1919	Republican Constitution adopted at Weimar. Treaty of Versailles.
1923	France occupies Ruhr. Attempted coup by Erich Ludendorff and Adolf Hitler in Munich.
1925	Paul von Hindenburg elected president. Germany admitted to League of Nations.
1929	World economic depression begins.
1933	Hitler becomes chancellor, is given full powers by Reichstag.
1934	Murder of Hitler's critics and opponents. Hindenburg dies; Hitler adds presidency to his other offices.
1936	German troops march into Rhineland in breach of Versailles treaty.
1938	Hitler seizes Austria. Munich agreement gives Sudetenland (part of Czechoslovakia) to Germany.
1939	Hitler seizes rest of Czechoslovakia and Memel (now Klaipeda, Lithuania). Hitler-Stalin pact. German invasion of Poland starts World War II.
1940	Germany occupies Denmark, Norway, Belgium, Netherlands, and France.
1941	Germany occupies Yugoslavia and Greece and invades Soviet Union. United States, attacked by Japan, enters war.
1942	German defeats at Alamein and Stalingrad.
1944	Allied landings in France. Unsuccessful plot against Hitler.
1945	Hitler, defeated, kills himself. German forces surrender. Potsdam Declaration lays down principles for occupation of Germany.
1948-1949	Soviet blockade of West Berlin.
1949	Federal Republic of Germany constituted at Bonn with Konrad Adenauer as chancellor. German Democratic Republic constituted in East Berlin.
1953	Death of Stalin. Rising in East Germany suppressed by Soviet Army.
1955	West Germany joins North Atlantic Treaty Organization. East Germany joins Warsaw Pact.
1956	Soviet Army suppresses Hungarian uprising.
1957	Incorporation of Saarland into West Germany after plebiscite.
1958	European Common Market established; West Germany founder member.
1959	West German Social Democratic Party adopts Godesburg program, accepting West European integration.
1961	Berlin Wall built.
1963	Franco-German treaty of cooperation.
1966	"Grand Coalition" of Christian Democrats and Social Democrats in Bonn.
1968	Student riots in West German cities: Bundestag passes emergency decree. Warsaw Pact forces invade Czechoslovakia to suppress "Prague Spring." Dissident Communist Robert Havermann protests in East Germany, is placed under house arrest.
1969	Willi Brandt, Social Democrat, becomes West Ger-

man chancellor; start of *Ostpolitik*.

1970	Four Powers Agreement on Berlin signed. Brandt visits East Germany; Council of Ministers President Willi Stoph visits West Germany. West German treaties with Soviet Union and Poland.
1972	*Grundlagenvertrag*: first treaty between East and West Germany on "basis of relations"; numerous other sectoral agreements (transport, energy, environment, etc.) in following years.
1973	Both Germanys become members of United Nations.
1974	Helmut Schmidt succeeds Brandt as chancellor.
1975	Helsinki Accords of Conference on Security and Cooperation in Europe signed by all European countries (except Albania), as well as United States and Canada.
1976	Wolf Biermann exiled from East Germany. Crackdown on dissent by intellectuals.
1977	Peak of Baader-Meinhof gang terrorism, supported by East German secret services. Rudolf Bahro publishes *The Alternative* in West Germany, is jailed in East on charges of espionage.
1978	Church-state agreement in East Germany.
1979	NATO decision to install short-range nuclear missiles.
1980	Schmidt visits Moscow.
1981	Major peace demonstrations in West Germany. Schmidt meets Erich Honecker in East Germany. Martial law in Poland outlaws Solidarity.
1982	Christian Democrat/Free Democrat coalition led by Helmut Kohl replaces Schmidt government but continues *Ostpolitik* with new agreements on trade, travel, environment.
1983	Trade credit of one billion DM from West Germany to East Germany. East Germany removes automatic firing devices at inter-German border (but maintains shoot-to-kill orders).
1984	Refugees use West German representation in East Berlin as sanctuary to travel west. New trade credit of almost one billion DM. East Germany eases travel restrictions.
1985	Mikhail Gorbachev assumes power in Soviet Union.
1986	Honecker visits West Germany.
1987	Hungarian Communist reformers call for new constitution, reducing role of party.
1988	Dissidents protest at Rosa Luxemburg demonstration in East Berlin. Honecker visits Moscow, claiming to support Gorbachev's reforms.
1989	**May.** Local elections in East Germany rigged in favor of Communists. Protests by church and dissident groups. Austrian and Hungarian foreign ministers cut barbed-wire fence dividing their countries.

June. Polish elections return Solidarity majority.

July, August. East German citizens seek refuge in West German embassies in Prague, Budapest and Warsaw, wanting to emigrate.

August. Tadeusz Mazowiecki becomes first non-Communist prime minister in a Soviet-bloc country.

September. Hungary officially opens border to Austria, denounces agreement with East Germany. Mass exodus of East German citizens. New Forum founded.

October. Official celebrations of forty-year anniversary of founding of East Germany. Gorbachev in Berlin. Honecker resigns. Egon Krenz new party leader. Hans Modrow heads government. Corruption scandals weaken party.

November. Over one million people demonstrate in East Berlin for freedom and elections. Communist leadership orders opening of Berlin Wall. Kohl offers ten-point-plan for unification.

December. Communist Party's right to leading role in society removed by East German parliament. Krenz resigns. Gregor Gysi new party leader. Roundtable talks called by church to involve government and opposition groups.

1990	**January-February.** New political parties active in East Germany.

March. Elections won by Conservative Alliance; joined in coalition by Social Democrats. New government agrees on program for unification to be negotiated with West Germany.

July. Treaty on Economic, Monetary and Social Union.

August. Collapse of East German economy despite monetary union. Social Democrats withdraw from East Berlin coalition.

September. Treaty on Political Union. "Two-plus-four" treaty signed in Moscow.

October. Regional (*Länder*) elections in East Germany, followed by formal unification.

December. All-German elections scheduled.

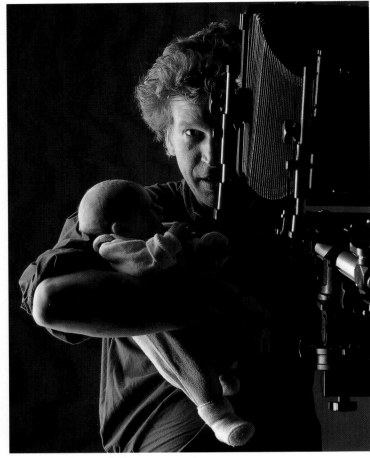

VOLKER DÖRING

Volker Döring was born thirty-seven years ago in East Berlin, and became a teacher before turning himself into a gifted photographer. He had hardly traveled west of the Wall before we asked him to share his first impressions of West Germany with us through his camera. The photographs he produced give a view of the West as seen with Eastern eyes.

JONS MICHAEL VOSS

Jons Michael Voss was born in 1956 in Hamburg, where he studied photography before moving to West Berlin to work. To gather his part of this tale, Voss traveled throughout East Germany to meet his soon-to-be fellow citizens and show us the human side of the political, economic, and social questions that unification is posing. He dedicated his contribution to this book to "my daughter, Zoe Charlotte, born the 4th of September, 1990. She will never see the 'good old' East Germany her mother came from."

EAST AND WEST
CONTRASTS AND SIMILARITIES
A Photographic View

Beauty lies in the eye of the beholder; so, too, does the critical spirit. When the East German photographer toured the West and his West German colleague toured the East, they each found memorable and striking images — some to admire, others to inspire sadness. The balance is by no means all in favor of one side, with everything in the West to be emulated and everything in the East to be regretted.

East German cars, trains, and housing were and are second-class compared to their West German equivalents. But all that glitters is not gold. While the glossy facade of Western society speaks eloquently of the material riches of West Germany, it also points to the temptation to put a hard-currency price tag on the quality of life. The photographers were concerned to show not just the skin-deep surface of the countries they visited, but also the way of life the people lead there.

That is what makes this visual record at once so fascinating and so valuable. The photographs capture the faces and gestures of ordinary people going through their daily paces — at work, at school, in their leisure hours, in public, and in the privacy of their own homes. Taken during 1990 in the last months of East Germany's existence as a separate country, the photographs are a telling memorial to a way of life in transition.

On the following pages scenes from East and West are placed opposite each other, with captions that fill in the background, so that the reader can make comparisons and draw his or her own conclusions. The photographs lend themselves to insights and reflections on the character of the German people who lived on different sides of the Iron Curtain.

As a wise observer commented to me when I went to work in Berlin in the 1980s, the people in these two countries have more in common as Germans than ever divided them ideologically. They have seen regimes come and go, have conquered and been conquered themselves; beneath all the political changes there is a continuity of shared experience that reaches back further than one person's lifetime.

Now political changes are converging with that experience, bringing together two parts of a nation that have been separate for almost two generations. When the symbols of East Germany are all taken down and the nation stands united beneath one banner, as German faces German, what will we see more — the contrasts or the similarities?

Hot summers bring Germans — West and East — out onto the streets and squares to watch the world go by. The Neptune Fountain in East Berlin's Alexanderplatz is a traditional spot for lovers; sitting under the hammer-and-compass symbol of the Communist state to read a Western magazine is less conventional. In the West, small towns and villages often have traditional May trees decorated with figures representing folklore symbols and local history. Modern sculpture has a sense of humor, and can add as much fun as art to the local scene.

Whether you're in a Western or an Eastern bar, beer is the standard drink, often with schnapps as a chaser. But soda is moving in fast, as many younger people decline alcohol. A mixture of Bohemian and traditional culture colors the streets in the West, where street musicians of all strains add their sounds to the traffic. Until recently, public military parades would march in the East, and the changing of the goose-stepping guards at East Berlin's memorial to the victims of fascism was a tourist attraction. Normal, too, is this civil defense exercise in an East Berlin suburb.

Street scenes in East and West display a contrast of generations. In the West, there is also a contrast of classes. Commuters, workers, pensioners . . . parents and children attend a left-wing demonstration while a bust of Lenin is sold second-hand. In the East, singers warm up for a makeshift pop concert. The baby-carriage-pushers are out demonstrating for women's rights, which are more liberal in the East. Young men just drafted for military service can beam because they know it won't last long now that the Wall is down. For some oldtimers in the service of the Communist state, the passing of the old order evokes a tear.

Private ownership of shops and a well-run apprentice-ship system ensure the survival of quality shops in West Germany, even for staple products like bread and meat. Open markets are still a normal shopping routine, and quality produce in the markets can rival what's on offer in the supermarkets. In the East the state-owned shops are no match for private markets, despite the heavy subsidies the shops receive to keep the cost of basic foodstuffs low. Unification is quickly eliminating these subsidies, and East Germans now have to pay much higher prices. But in many cases they prefer to spend even more to buy Western produce rather than buy the same quality from an East German source at a lower price.

SHOPPING

Toys and fashions exemplify the West's oversupply of consumer goods. Both items have a high degree of built-in obsolescence. Modern shopping centers are capitalism's temples to consumerism, but they are matched by the counterculture's open-air markets. If West Germany is a "throw-away" society, East Germany relied on "make do and mend." For shoe repairs, carried out while you wait in the privacy of a converted house, customers line up patiently outside. In outdoor markets housewives inspect rolls of cloth to make their own clothes and furnishings, while an enterprising private East German fashion designer tries to sell her styles outside the state distribution system.

With unification East Germans are being exposed to the shocks of the consumer society for the first time. Before they could see Western television ads, but they were protected from the reality of the West's materialism. They were tied to a command economy which produced in response to orders from above, not in response to consumer demand. The traditional shops

and small stores, almost all run by the state distribution service, now face real competition from Western retailers who have moved into the East German market. First to feel the squeeze were newsstands and newspapers. Circulation of Communist party papers slumped when the Wall came down as people flocked to buy Western papers from improvised stands.

Showrooms in West Germany gleam with variety, choice, pizzazz, and the latest high performance models while rows of East German Trabants — design and performance virtually·unchanged for a generation — await collection in the East. Delivery of the ubiquitous and highly priced "Trabis" could take up to ten years for rank-and-file citizens. So despite poor performance, they brought even higher prices secondhand. Once the Wall fell, the Trabant production line closed down. Even in the chaotic times after currency union, Easterners preferred to pay out for used Western cars sold expensively on the black market.

Bikers show enthusiasm and admiration for faster, sleeker, more powerful models in the West, while sobriety and practicality are hallmarks of the designs offered in the East. Even if the bike isn't speedy, it can keep you dry while you put-put out to the Karl Marx kitchen-garden plots to supplement the family's food with home-grown produce.

If unification progresses as planned, the near empty highways in the East will soon fill up. Both Germanys are crowded countries — 60 million in the West and 16 million in the East — yet both could fit together into Texas, so public transport is more efficient and economic than private cars. Buses, trolleys, and trains are common in both countries, even if East German rolling stock is old and some of the locomotives still run on steam. But highly subsidized fares in the East are disappearing as the two economies are brought together.

Work is work: these studies of Germans at their daily jobs in East and West show the mixture of pride and concentration you can find everywhere. What differs is the social context. Industry in East Germany was organized in 137 *Kombinate*, the equivalent of a major conglomerate in the West. It was through a job in one of these that workers had access to housing and other social benefits. Only a few thousand individuals in

the whole country were licensed to work as independent craftsmen, supplying goods and services to whomever was prepared to pay for them. Their contribution to the economy was what the central planners could not easily foresee or control. For ideological reasons the number of independents was kept to a minimum, though demand for their services and their goods was endless.

Differences between East and West show up more clearly in large-scale industry. Efficient, state-of-the-art production in the West contrasts with under-capitalized, antiquated processes in the East. There are exceptions like Karl Zeiss optics at Jena and specialist areas such as open-cast lignite mining. But even here the common complaint against the Communists is that they ran the country down economically. Safety margins were reduced, maintenance was cut. As a result breakdowns became common, production was lost, and quality declined. Now many factories and even some power plants will have to close; they have become either uneconomic or unsafe, or both. Workers in East German factories had a ready quip to explain the relation between low productivity and low wages: "They pretend to pay us — and we pretend to work."

Western front offices may be computerized and pleasant places to work, but dirty jobs and anti-social shifts still abound in contemporary society. In West Germany many of these are taken by immigrants, for close to one worker in seven is a *Gastarbeiter* or guest worker, often from Turkey, Yugoslavia, or North Africa. Now they are being displaced by ethnic Germans coming from all over Eastern Europe and the Soviet Union. The new immigrants are often people with inadequate command of the German language and skills poorly adapted to a modern industrial society. East German industry needed little additional labor. With high unemployment looming on the unification horizon, the few Poles, North Koreans and Vietnamese who were there are now being repatriated. Managing a demotivated workforce with out-of-date equipment in a centrally planned economy had few professional rewards; now competition with the West could put both managers and workers out of a job.

As unification proceeds, East German firms will feel the full blast of West German competition. The governments have jointly set up the *Treuhandstelle* in Berlin to break up the *Kombinate* and rescue whatever parts they can. With unemployment likely to top 20 percent and more than one company in five due to be scrapped, the task is daunting. Their aim is to marry up Western companies with East German firms. But problems arise in deciding just who owns the Eastern firms, as many have grown from private companies expropriated after World War II or during Communist compaigns to nationalize industry. As all this goes on, Gorbachev looks out from a poster upon a typical out-of-date office where a typical out-of-date Communist party notice exhorts members to organize better.

West German farmers mostly work family farms, but they are no strangers to modern methods and machinery and have reaped huge benefits from the European Community's Common Agricultural Policy. In the East, Communist policy began by distributing the estates of the old Prussian aristocracy among the peasantry, but only a few years later the regime took the land away again to make vast collective farms. The result was apathethic agricultural workers, poor productivity, and minimal capital investment.

A "Green" farming movement has grown in the West out of a concern for the environment and the higher prices offered for organic produce. Western agriculture is characterized by the drive for greater quality and variety, while in the East poor produce from the farms hardly feeds the population. Abundant Western food went on sale in Eastern shops after currency union, and demand for East German produce slumped. Some was shipped to the Soviet Union as food aid, but large quantities were destroyed. East German agriculture is now in crisis. The old fashioned distribution infrastructure — like this ferry — is ripe to become a tourist attraction.

"Costs up, prices down. Germany's farmers face ruin," says the sign beside the vines. But West German wines sell well worldwide, and the countryside exudes quiet prosperity. Family farms are not large — less than 100 acres on average — but are well run. In East Germany, on the other hand, collectivization has deprived farmers of pride in their own land. Young people go to the towns as soon as possible, leaving the villages ever less lively.

Pollution knows no frontiers and Germans East and West have a bad mess to clean up. Water, air, and soil pollution all present major problems to industry and government. Efforts at recycling — for environmental reasons in the West, out of economic need in the East — go some way toward conserving scarce resources, but the size of the problem in the heartland of Europe's economic miracle is daunting. East Germany's reliance on low grade lignite from open-cast mines has scarred the countryside and blackened the towns. As the environmental damage became obvious in the 1980s, ecology movements grew and in the end contributed to the body of dissidents who eventually changed the system.

Acid rain, polluted shorelines, dead rivers, untreated effluent, and dying wildlife — all are aspects of the degraded environment in the two Germanys. Protesters post a banner saying the chemical industry is turning the living earth into a dead moon. Many East German factories will have to close unless they can adapt quickly to environmental standards agreed upon by all the member governments of the European Community. Cleaning up unified Germany will be a long and very expensive job.

ENVIRONMENT

Strict building regulations and buoyant demand have given West Germany well planned, modern housing developments on the outskirts of its major cities. Most houses and apartments are privately owned, but the prices are high. Rent or the mortgage is usually the largest single item in a family's budget. Not so in East

Germany, where housing is owned by the government and subsidies keep rents very low. New building has not kept pace with demand and several generations can still be found sharing one apartment. But plenty of parks, child-care centers, and playgrounds are provided, even if living space indoors is cramped.

Across the Germanys you can see a wide variety of building styles for family homes. Thatched roofs are traditional in some regions, but also considered chic for new houses trying to appear rich and rural. Garden sheds and summer homes are another common way of getting a little closer to nature, whichever side of the border you are on. Rents in the East have been frozen since 1950, so the few remaining private landlords have no incentive to maintain property there. But where someone has built their own rural retreat, the care lavished on it can even compare favorably with country houses in the West.

Whether they're escaping from the economic stress of work in the capitalist West or the political strain of coping with the regime in the Communist East, in the family circle the common German character reasserts itself. At Christmas and birthday feasts that bring families together, or while visiting grandma on Sunday for cakes and coffee, talking with parents one evening, or enjoying the garden with young Hermann, there is little that visibly distinguishes West from East. The barge captain with his young son, the student washing at the pump, and the father setting off with his family on bicycles are all engaged in activities quite normal for the German "tribe."

Although the Germans are the largest single language group in Europe, the birth rate is currently too low to replace the numbers of those who die. In the West contraception is readily available while the East has liberal abortion laws. Germans have a reputation of

not being keen on children; statistics show that many couples prefer to spend more on housing and cars rather than have another child. Grandparents often help care for children, playing and teaching, and this can add a special continuity with the past.

Kids will be kids and at an early age nothing can stifle their ebullient energy, even when they're playing in "no man's land" within sight of the graffiti-scrawled Wall. For children in the West there is an oversupply of teachers, many of whom can find no work. In the East the teaching profession was almost completely Communist. All pupils had compulsory classes of Marxism-Leninism and school books for every subject were used as a basis for political indoctrination. In a united Germany politicized teachers from the East may yet cause problems for a Western tradition that tries to keep politics out of the schools.

The younger generation distances itself from its parents by its dress and appearance first, and then by its behavior, by what it does. West Berlin attracted many young men — some as students, some as dropouts — since while they lived there they were exempt from being drafted into the West German army. Not so in East Germany, where very few young men were even allowed to serve in non-combatant companies if they objected to military service on conscientious grounds. High-spirited youngsters could easily find themselves in court for "rowdy behavior." Bringing the national flag into disrepute would not have been tolerated before the collapse of the old regime. Now draping yourself in it is simply a gesture of non-conformism.

Although blue jeans may be the informal uniform of youth in East and West, formal dress still plays a big role in East Germany. At "youth initiation" ceremonies and graduations, bouquets and bow ties are the norm. Only the conformist children of politically reliable parents were given places at universities. But both societies provide plenty of private opportunities for young people to meet. In the West it is often in commercial settings, like clubs and discotheques; in the East settings are organized by the party, the school, or the church. International pop stars sing to a common following in both Germanys and you find the same pin-ups across the land, but the pop-culture traffic is essentially one way, from West to East.

YOUTH

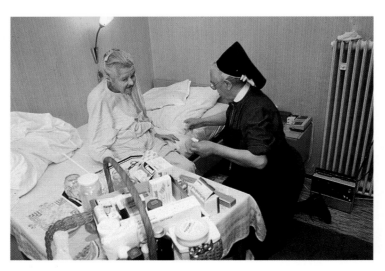

Old people are the memory of a nation. These old people are near contemporaries of Hitler; their parents were contemporaries of Bismarck. Scores of thousands of retired East Germans came to the West throughout the 1970s and 1980s. The West German government offered to pay their pensions and the East German government had no objection to the elderly leaving the country once their economically productive years were past. Many people made the move to rejoin their families, separated since the end of World War II; others came knowing they would face their declining years in solitude but with a higher standard of living. For instance, telephones, which can be a lifeline for the elderly, are common in the West, but only seven in a hundred have a phone in East Germany.

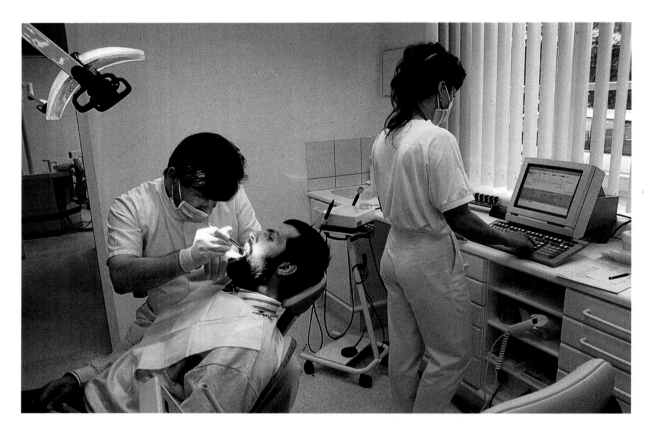
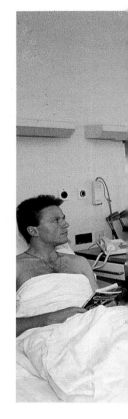

Health care in West Germany is financed by personal insurance and does not lack resources. State-of-the-art technology aids diagnosis and treatment; pharmacies are well stocked and medicines are widely available. With considerably fewer resources East Germany finances its health system by public subsidy, making treatment free or virtually free to the patient. But a system meeting great demand with few resources inevitably has less modern equipment and will present a more outdated image, even if the quality of patient care remains high. Now young doctors from West Germany, where more are trained than can be employed, are being encouraged to move to the East to help fill the big gaps left by those who fled from Communist rule during the second half of 1989.

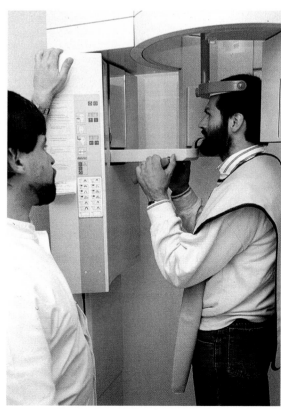

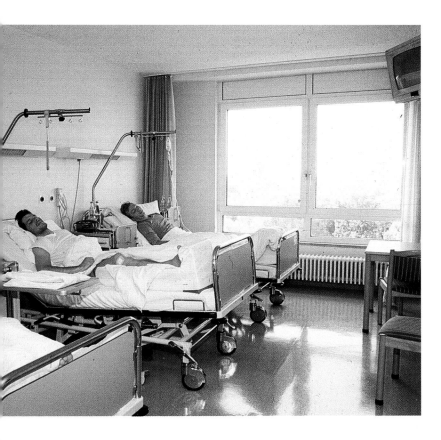

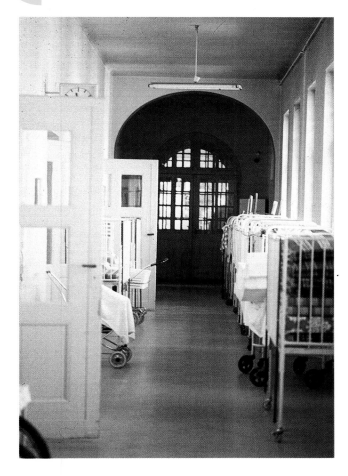

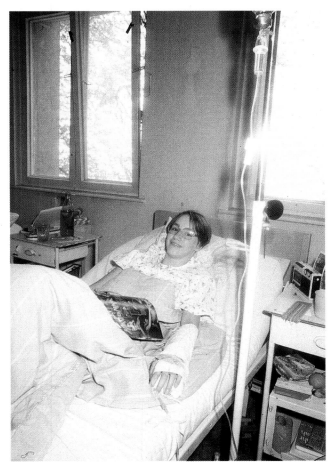

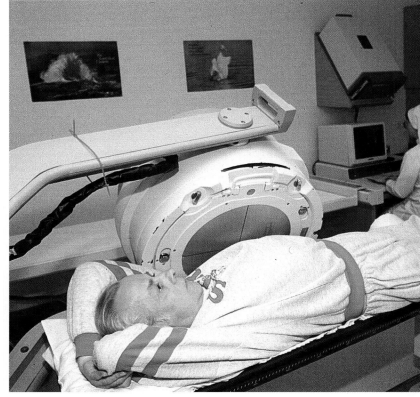

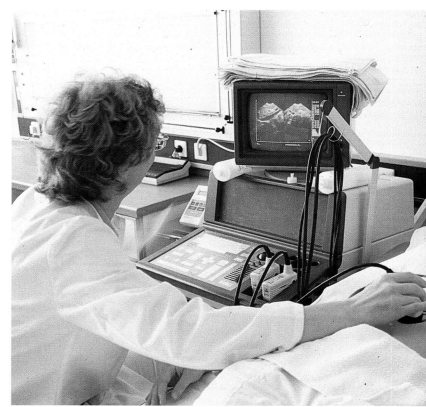

In both East and West the churches are involved in health care, sometimes providing complete hospitals. In the West their provision parallels that of the public authorities, while in the East it is designed to be complementary, dovetailing with undermanned or under-resourced services in the public sector. Some medical specialties in the East rival Western practice — heart surgery and skin grafting in Berlin, for instance — but they are exceptions. Most doctors work in old buildings with minimal resources and are not as well paid in relation to other professions as their West German counterparts are. That's one reason many of them fled to the West.

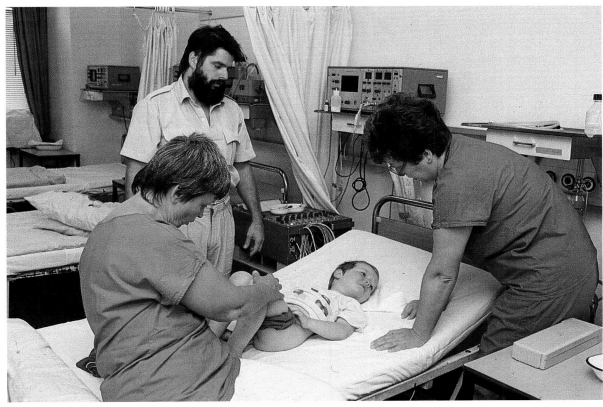

Church taxes in West Germany ensure an adequate income to maintain existing churches and build new ones. Not so in East Germany, where several churches have been left to decay beyond repair, despite generous help from the West. Yet the outward signs of church activity, in particular the poor state of many buildings, belie the quality of religious life there. Under Communism in the East, the churches were a rallying point for all those who could not identify with the atheistic regime. In sermons and discussion groups concerned with peace, the environment, and human rights, dissent crystalized into opposition, and churchmen found themselves answering a second calling — playing political roles as the old Communist order collapsed.

From the baroque splendor of the Catholic south to the austere Protestant churches of the north, religion plays a major role in German social life. Old traditions in Bavaria, like wood carving, are filled with a simple religious faith. There are 23 million Catholics in West Germany and 25 million Protestants. Political affiliation partly follows this division, with Christian Democrats and their Christian Social allies strong in traditional Catholic areas while the Social Democrats' strength has traditionally been more in Protestant lands. In East Germany there are only one million Catholics but more than four million Protestants.

Going to the theater or a concert is a social outing in both Germanys, but the splendor of the halls obviously differs. Both states heavily subsidize their showcase theater, opera, and ballet companies to boost their international standing. Only pop can and does survive without public money, drawing vast crowds in East and West. East German theater had added spice

when a turn of phrase, a piece of costume, or a particular gesture could acquire political meaning. Several famous cabaret revues served as social safety valves, where audiences could laugh at political jokes the censors had approved. They could criticize the system with an eye to improving the way it worked, but never lampoon the leadership in person. That was taboo.

In the West the public has long been used to modernism in the visual arts. Individual expression is at a premium while social relevance is, at best, secondary. In contrast the annual art exhibition of the Union of Graphic Artists in East Germany was a political barometer, a touchstone of the ideological climate. If the Communist authorities were opening up to the West, some abstract sculptures and paintings would be displayed. If they were clamping down on Western contacts, only examples of Socialist realism would be selected, depicting the positive side of themes from Communist history or representatives of the proletariat. With the Wall no longer dividing the artistic world of the Germans, artists previously subsidized by the government in the East will enjoy a new aesthetic freedom — but they may lose their immediate relevance to society and have to compete for commissions in the marketplace.

With Boris Becker and Stefi Graf as international stars, tennis has taken off in West Germany. But it is not a cheap sport and private instruction is reserved for those who can afford it. In East Germany the government subsidized sport heavily and collected nearly as many Olympic medals as the Soviet Union, thanks to a system which identified talent early and trained it intensively. International competitions were used as a showcase for sporting achievements that would bring glory to the Communist government.

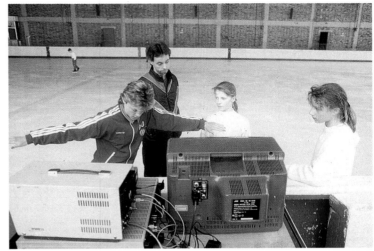

Soccer is the most popular sport, East and West. Winning the World Cup in 1990 made Chancellor Kohl almost as happy as seeing reunification under his leadership. But the West German professional soccer league involves big money, and the East cannot compete at that level. In economic crisis, East Germany has to retrench, dismissing thousands of trainers for a variety of sports. Stars are losing their privileges, such as Western cars, larger apartments, and foreign travel. In future, youngsters will have to find a route to international fame without government backing.

The neon lights are brighter in the West. There are more discotheques, nightclubs, and mindless machine amusements. In East Germany evening entertainment is less commercialized and still mainly family centered. Young people feel cramped in both cultures by their elders, but in the West they can escape to the company of their peers much more easily than in the East.

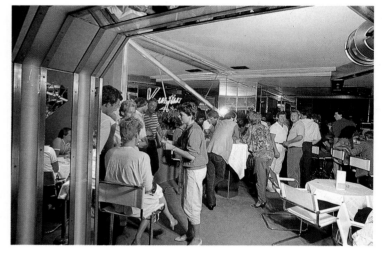

There is a formality about East German society that has been lost in the West. Put the other way around, there is an informality in the West that the East has not yet learned. It's not only the bright lights and famous skyline landmarks of West Berlin that make its nightlife different from the East. West Germans are considered gregarious by other Northern Europeans. But in East Germany there is an attitude of mind that is more restrained, and not just by the strict enforcement of an absolute ban on drinking and driving.

127

The Palace of the Republic was the East German government's showpiece in East Berlin. The old castle was torn down to clear the site beside the Spree in the center of the city; now the building houses several restaurants, the parliament's debating chamber, a theater, and convention rooms. But its chrome, glass, and steel decor — impressive in the 1960s — seems odd and cold compared to the cosy *Gemutlichkeit* of a Western café-bar where old friends gather to play Skat, a traditional card game, and dance to golden oldies tunes. Casinos now abound in the West, and stakes can be high. But in the Palace of the Republic gambling is strictly forbidden.

Since Turnvater Jahn founded a nationalist movement based on physical fitness in the early nineteenth century, Germans have admired and taken pride in physically healthy bodies. All ages, shapes, and sizes in both Germanys take part in a wide range of sports and physical activities, though the style sometimes differs sharply. Simpler and less expensive leisure pursuits can tax the mind, like open-air chess in a West German park, or even lead to much prized foreign travel, as for this East German dog lover. Winners' medals line the walls of his apartment and show he traveled throughout Eastern Europe — but only the *East* — to bring home prizes to his country.

If God really is a gardener, as some traditions suggest, then Germans are made in his image. The garden is a place to tend and care for, to display with pride, to sit in and enjoy. Plant nurseries are thriving businesses in both Germanys, for visitors know a plant or flowers are always welcomed presents. As new apartment complexes expand the cities, so land is set aside for allotments, both in the East and the West. It is a tradition linked to the rapid growth of German cities at the end of the last century, when workers needed a plot of land to help feed their families and to keep in touch with their rural roots. A shed, a summer home, or just a table and chairs can transform a place of hard physical work into a corner where urbanites can get away, relax, and enjoy good company.

Wanderlust takes millions of rich West Germans abroad each summer, especially south to the sunshine beaches of the Mediterranean. Until recently, most East Germans had to be content with what their own land could offer, since travel even to neighboring East European countries was increasingly restricted during the 1980s. The equipment — yachts, gliders, sailboards — is more plentiful, colorful, and sophisticated in the West, but that does not stop East Germans from enjoying themselves.

East or West you need sunshine to bring the seaside to life. And when the sun does shine on the North Sea or the Baltic coast, Germans in their thousands flock to the beach. Since travel abroad was almost impossible, overcrowding on the East German stretch of the Baltic in the 1980s became so bad that drinking water ran short. Four million holiday-makers overloaded facilities designed to cope with only half that number. The moveable blue "huts" and wicker baskets look so alike and serve the same purpose: beach "home" for the day.

Differences in material standards show up clearly when you look at camping grounds, trailers, and hotels in East and West Germany. Luxurious trailers pulled by Mercedes sedans arrive at groomed sites in the West; Easterners on this sort of holiday make do with more primitive conditions. Hotels with restaurants, like this converted Alpine chalet, polka-dot the Western countryside and cater for tourists at a high standard. Until recently this weatherworn Eastern institutional hotel owned by the Communist-dominated Trade Union Federation, like many of its ilk, catered only for groups of its own members.

Away from the coast, Germany enjoys a continental climate with bitterly cold winters but gloriously hot summers. Then life comes outdoors, open-air cafés abound, and there is entertainment for everyone — from town bands playing at a wedding in an Alpine village to magicians mystifying children in a Berlin park. In the West it's easier to find a place to be alone, either enjoying a beer or brooding on life's injustices, but in the East the older generation or Big Brother always seemed to be there in the background.

Two Into One:
Reactions to Unification

Europe is a small, densely populated place. Germany's central position means all its neighbors are vitally concerned about what happens in that country. Their concern is fueled as much by fear as by admiration. The French author François Mauriac put it bluntly when he wrote: "I love Germany so much I prefer to see two of them." Bitter memories linger, tempering enthusiasm about the unification of Germany. As the Cold War melts into memory, some politicians are eagerly looking for popular ways to spend the "peace dividend," but others are hanging back, realizing that the changes also fuel old fears of Germany.

Many people feel awed by German achievements. They admire Germany's economic success and its cultural and intellectual traditions. Others recall with fear and horror the excesses of German arrogance, the brutality of military conquest and racial subjugation, the cold efficiency and inhumanity of planned extermination.

Germany arouses strong passions and prejudices. It is, in the popular saying, *Das Land der Dichter und Denker*, the land of poets and philosophers, but also *Das Land der Richter und Henker*, the land of judges and executioners.

"History," wrote Edward Gibbon in the 18th century, is "little more than the register of the crimes, follies, and misfortunes of mankind." Had he turned his powerful mind to the history of Germany and viewed the subject at the end of the 20th century, he might have come to the same conclusion. Germany's fate has been central to the fate of Europe for more than a hundred years, and its history has been marked by more than its fair share of crimes, follies, and misfortunes. But German history has also been European history. When you see the map of Europe, you cannot overlook Germany.

Three irreversible facts have emerged from the recent turmoil in Europe. First is the collapse of Communism as a system of government and as a system of belief. Not for a long time, if ever again, will collectivist ideas steer the societies of Eastern Europe. They are set on course for democracy, for individual rights and freedoms.

Second is the withdrawal of Soviet military and political influence. The Soviet Union has no central role to play in the day-to-day running of the newly independent countries of the Eastern bloc. Gone are the days when the Soviet ambassador was the most powerful man in their land.

Third is the fact of German unification. East and West Germany will unite to become the dominant country in Central Europe. We have grown so used to living with a divided and weakened Germany that we forget that since Bismarck's time Germany has been the dominant power in that part of Europe. Lenin spoke a bitter truth when he said, "Whoever holds Berlin holds Germany. Whoever holds Germany holds Europe."

Fears of a united Germany are based on three key factors: population, economic strength, and the past.

There simply are more Germans than any other nationality in Europe: sixty-one million people live in the West and sixteen million in the East. The United Kingdom has fifty-six million people, Italy fifty-five million, France fifty-two million, Spain and Poland thirty-five million each. Although the birth rate is falling, Germany will maintain its population lead. It has and will continue to have more human resources at its disposal than any other country in Europe.

Part of the fear of a unified Germany stems from its economic power. History is full of ironies, and one of the richest contemporary ironies is the fact that the defeated nations of World War II, Germany and Japan, are now the economic victors. Per capita income in West Germany is considerably higher than in Britain or France. Its total gross national product measures close to one-third of the combined total for all twelve countries of the European Community. It has a trade surplus of over $70 billion, equal to more than half the United States' trade deficit. In addition, its gold and foreign currency reserves total more than $60 billion. True, unification will cost West Germany money initially: extra cash for social services in the East and a bailout for East Germany's public debt. There will also be slightly increased inflation, a marginal weakening of the Deutsche Mark. But once private investment is under way in the East, there will be a positive return. No one doubts that the economic strength of the united Germany will make it by far the strongest power in Europe. The neighboring countries, in East as well as West, want to keep this growing giant well-integrated into the European Community and NATO, anchored into the existing patterns of joint decision-making in economic and military matters.

Current attitudes are partly formed by experience of the past. France, Britain, Spain, and the Netherlands expanded overseas to found colonies and rule empires, but Germany came on the scene as a European power too late to spread its influence in other continents. Instead it concentrated on territorial and cultural expansion in Europe, notably Eastern Europe. Germany's neighbors, especially the Slavic countries of Eastern Europe, experienced the brutality of German domination. Old attitudes of cultural and at times ethnic superiority fuel fears among Germany's neighbors. Old attitudes belong to a past that everyone hopes the Germans have put behind them, but all Europeans, including the Germans, secretly wonder whether newfound German pride in a unified country will revive old views of superiority.

The fear of a united Germany is also a question of generations. Older people remember all the horrors of war. The past has left an indelible mark on them. Younger people, if aware of the horrors at all, know them only through films and books, lessons at school, and the tales told by their parents and grandparents. This is as true in Germany as in neighboring countries. In Germany the problems of guilt and innocence, complicity and acquiescence have to be worked out by each individual, and inevitably some are more thorough and conscientious than others. Insofar as the state, and hence the schools, can further this process, the peaceful revolution in the East marks a major positive step. The first official act of the new East German government was to publicly acknowledge German responsibility for the Holocaust, in which millions of political opponents, Jews, Gypsies, homosexuals, handicapped people, and others were murdered in accordance with government policy. Responsibility for the deeds of the past was consistently denied by the former Communist government, which argued that it was no successor to the fascist regime of the Nazis. So only now, forty-five years after the defeat of Hitler's Reich, can East Germans begin honestly and publicly coming to terms with their nation's history.

Despite reservations, all of Germany's neighbors rejoice that the Cold War obstacles to social and personal contact between the two Germanys have been removed. The Berlin Wall was a monument to inhumanity. Now what awaits us all is the experiment of unification, bringing together two parts that are so different, but so similar.

Yet in their enthusiasm for the freedoms of the West, East Germans may find they have imported disadvantages as well. The visible evils of consumerism, crime, unemployment, and pornography are obvious, but the breakdown of the spirit of solidarity that bound together friends, neighbors, even whole communities in the difficult task of living under an unloved system may prove a hidden casualty of the successful revolution. The East Germans' consolation will be to know that the virtues they displayed in adversity are no longer necessary in a democratic, pluralist Germany that respects the greater rights and freedoms they struggled successfully to achieve.

PHOTO CREDITS

TL: Top Left   T: Top   TR: Top Right
ML: Mid-Left   M: Middle   MR: Mid-Right
BL: Bottom Left   B: Bottom   BR: Bottom Right

Archiv für Kunst und Geschichte
P. 10   BR
P. 12   TR
P. 13   ALL
P. 14   TL   ML
P. 15   ALL
P. 16   TL
P. 17   TM   BL   BR
P. 18   BR
P. 19   ALL
P. 20   ML   BL
P. 21   ALL
P. 22   TR
P. 23   TL   BL
P. 24   ALL
P. 25   BL   BR
P. 26   ALL
P. 27   ALL
P. 28   ALL
P. 29   ALL
P. 30   BL
P. 31   BL
P. 35   ALL
P. 45   MR
P. 49   ML

Archiv Gerstenberg
P. 17   TR
P. 22-23 M
P. 22   BR
P. 30   TR

Jürgens Photo
P. 10   BL
P. 34   ML
P. 38   TL
P. 39   ALL EXCEPT TR
P. 41   ALL
P. 42   TL

Carolina Salguero, EXYS
P. 44   MR
P. 45   BR
P. 46   ML
P. 47   ALL
P. 49   TL   BL

Jan-Peter Böning, EXYS
P. 2-3   ALL
P. 39   TR
P. 45   TR
P. 48   TL   TR
P. 49   TR   MR   BR

Associated Press
P. 38   ML   MR
P. 43   ALL
P. 48   BL

Volker Döring
P. 42   ML

German Tourist Board
P. 12   TL

All photos on pp. 54-141, except as listed below, are
from Volker Döring (photos of West Germany) and
Jons Michael Voss (photos of East Germany):

Bilderberg Archiv der Fotografen
P. 88   MR
P. 89   BL

The Environmental Picture Library
P. 88   TR

Greenpeace Communications Ltd.
P. 88   BR
P. 90   TL   TR   ML   MR
P. 91   BR

Horstmüller
P. 120   TL   TR
P. 121   TL   ML   MR   BR